Wealth Building Secrets From Warren Buffett Annual Shareholder Meetings

Bill Glaser

B&C Publishing

Published by B&C Publishing
1135 Country Club Drive
Minden, NV 89423-8855

ISBN 978-0-9824088-0-3

Printed in the United States

Chapter 1

It was the first Saturday in May, 1998. My wife, Cheryl, and I arrived at Ak-Sar-Ben Coliseum at 6:30 a.m., excited to be going to our first Berkshire Hathaway Annual Shareholder Meeting in Omaha, Nebraska, and, especially to see and hear Warren Buffett. It was a sunny, but cool morning.

There was already a line of about 50 people waiting to get into the Coliseum. The doors were scheduled to open at 7:00 a.m. At about 6:40 a.m., an older grey car drove past our line and pulled up to the back of the Colisium, and out jumped Warren. What a surprise! And, even more surprising, was that he was driving himself! Warren quickly disappeared into the building.

Ak-Sar-Ben has since been torn down, but at the time, it was a large complex located between 60th and 72nd streets, and between Center and Pacific streets, in the center of Omaha. At one time, Ak-Sar-Ben was a horse racetrack and an arena that held hockey matches, ice skating and rodeos. It held about 10,000 people.

There was an electricity of excited anticipation in the air as the line to the arena continued to grow behind us. Everyone chatted with people in line near them from other parts of the country (we had traveled from San Diego for the event), and we were no exception.

Since I grew up in Omaha, I was familiar with the town. I had been studying Warren Buffett and his accomplishments since 1984, but like most people, did not have extra money to invest in his stock—which, incidentally always seemed to be at an astronomically high price because Warren never split his stock (most large corporations split their stock when it goes above $100, to keep the price per share low, but not Warren).

The doors finally opened at 7:00 a.m., and the crowd charged in. As we also raced in the door hoping to get a good seat, we noticed a man standing against the wall amusedly observing the crowd racing to get the best seats. That man, of course, was Warren--watching with a secret smile on his face. Of those few who saw him, not one stopped to try to talk to him because they were afraid all the good seats would be gone.

After we got our seats (ten rows up and about one quarter of the way down the arena from the stage), we went to the concession stand where complementary coffee, rolls, Danishes, water, and Coca Cola were served.

After what seemed like an eternity, the meeting began. In those days the meeting began with the election of corporate officers. This, of course, took very little time because Warren controls a majority of the stock of Berkshire Hathaway (this part of the meeting now has been moved to the end).

Then the fun began — the question and answer period. Charlie Munger, the vice chairman of Berkshire Hathaway, and Warren sit on the stage at a very plain table and do a question-and-answer session with the audience from 9:30 a.m. to 3:00 p.m., with a short break for lunch. Microphones are set up around the arena where shareholders can ask questions. After Warren answers the question, he usually turns to Charlie to see if he wants to comment. Most of the time, Charlie looks like he is asleep, and we were always surprised to hear him say, "Nothing to add." He had really been listening all along. This always gets a big laugh from the audience.

The following is a summary of the question and answer session. Most of the comments are Warren's. Items in bold are what I thought to be most important.

Question: What makes the PE go up?

Warren: The PE ratio moves up because people think it (the company) is better. **Absolute move-up is based on earnings and interest rates.** Declining interest rates push up stocks.

We try not to do anything difficult.

We have looked at stocks in all markets. Japan businesses have low return on equity.

Time is the enemy of a poor business; it is the friend of a good business.

Berkshire was selling well below working capital.

Filters to analyze businesses and people.

Not interested in investing in technology as does not understand.

We have to allocate capital.

Question: How do you decide to sell?

Warren: **We buy stock; we don't want to sell.**

Question: Who chooses the colors for annual report?

Warren: I did red this year to honor Tom Osborne, the University of Nebraska Football Coach.

Our insurance business is the most important. I said many years ago that it would be.

Next came one of the most memorable moments of any of the eight annual meetings that we have attended. Both my wife's and my work thought mission statements were the basis of any well-run business.

Question: Does Berkshire have a mission statement?

Charlie: Stated, emphatically, **"I AM PROUD TO SAY WE HAVE NO MISSION STATEMENT!"** This brought howls of laughter and approving applause from the 9,000 shareholder attendees in the audience.

Question: On return on equity of banks – tangible equity.

Warren: I am unimpressed; unsustainable. 30% yes if retain most earnings ????

The secret to life is weak competition.

Jack Welsh of GE is mentioned as a good CEO.

Question: Charlie is asked about his book recommendations.

Charlie: He likes *Guns, Germs, and Steel*. He says to ask Why? Why? Why? Also likes *Quotable Einstein*.

Question: What keeps you awake at night?

Warren: We don't worry.

Charlie: We like the game. It's a lot of fun even in tough times. We are like undertakers during the plague.

Think about things that are important and knowable.

Warren stated that Coke sells 1 billion 8-ounce servings per day.

Value Line has 1,700 stocks to look at. We don't look at ratings. It only takes us 30 seconds to get the key information on a company.

Price action and volatility have nothing to do with what we do.

Question: Considering consolidation in insurance?

Warren: No problem; we have sensational insurance businesses.

Question: Should one buy back stock at high PE, 40.

Warren: No-bad time.

Warren went on to state that Coke is the best large business in the world. Berkshire owned 6.3% of Coke in 1988. With repurchase of stock by Coke, Berkshire share went to 8%. Good for Coke; but not for some other businesses.

Berkshire share of GEICO went from 33% to 50%, with GEICO repurchase of stock. Berkshire share of Washington Post went from 9% to 17%, with their repurchase of stock.

Insurance – Berkshire has $7 billion of float shown as a liability on the balance sheet, but it is really an asset. (Float in insurance is money that has been paid in to the company in premiums and not yet paid out in claims that can be used by the company for investments until needed.)

Charlie: Ask and then what????

Question: Japan dump treasuries?

Warren: No problem; somebody else buys. Sell - get us money, no threat.

We step over 1 foot bars; we do not try to jump over 8 foot bars.

Net exporter to U.S.

Question: This person studies New York real estate private investment accounts – 2% invest in index of stocks, 2% out of 12% don't drop benefit below 5/6 of current cost of capital for Berkshire Hathaway?

Charlie: How it is taught in business school is incoherent – it is a stupid question - we are drowning in cash.

Question: Will Berkshire declare a dividend?

Warren: The question seems to be whether to return money to shareholders or get return greater than $1 of value for every $1 retained. Answer seems self-evident.

We never had many stock recommendations from analysts; we don't want them.

Insurance is the most important business that we have - not just super cat (catastrophe) business.

Dumb competitors are the problem.

Coke adds 1.5 billion cases per year. GEICO policies are like cases of Coke. We look for predictability.

We look for the fat pitch.

Question: Is WESCO a Class C Berkshire?

Warren: No, WESCO is not a clone of Berkshire. We own 80% of WESCO

Many investors have unrealistic expectations.

You will do well if you buy at a good price and the business does well.

I play bridge ten hours a week. Charlie plays 3 to 4 hours a week.

Question: Disney accounting on buy ABC/Cap Cities?

Warren: No problem; earnings are higher than reported.

Question: Usual question regarding Berkshire purchasing Tech stocks.

Warren: I admire Grove (Andy Grove of Intel) and Gates (Bill Gates of Microsoft), but don't know where the company will be in ten years.

They (Tech) are 8 foot bars. I can't clear it. Better to swing at easy pitches.

Question: Do you plan to buy back Berkshire Hathaway shares?

Warren's Answer: Maybe, sometime ago, but got other stuff I

like better – I don't like to borrow money to buy back shares.

Question: Supply and demand – silver. Shortage of supply.

Charlie: 2% of assets not a big deal. Wait 30 years to invest 2% of assets.

Warren: I only talk to students.

I waited to buy a house from '52 to '56 – put down 10% of my net worth.

Paying a lot for mediocrity is bad. Good perform ok. Large sums per se don't bother me. System feeds on itself.

Question: Small cap vs large cap?

Warren: We don't look at that or sectors, or stuff that gets merchandised.

Sandy Weill (of Citigroup) is a very good manager.

We missed the drug industry.

Question: Do you get annual business plans from companies you own?

Warren: No formal system. No. We do meet with them informally. We let each manager go his own way.

Talent is a scarce commodity. When you find it – good.

What is the Intrinsic value of a company?

Warren: Discount at long rate, credit for net cash flow. **Best business - cash comes in, you don't have to spend cash to expand.**

Investing equals lay-out cash now to get cash back later.

EBITA is nonsense.

Question: What is the criteria used to select a stock or business?

Warren: Understand the product.

Earning power good and getting better.

Good people.

Good price.

Simple, but not easy.

Know what you don't know.

If you know the future, it is easy.

It is good to teach business from cases where the business decision or answer is easy. National Cash Register - Like companies that have character.

BRKA vs BRKB 1A=30B one way
B=1/30th of A - less voting in B; no charitable contributions in B.

Learn all the accounting you can. It is the language of business.

If the market goes down, we like it. We can buy more!

Work at a number of businesses; see how they work. What is the competition?

Read about businesses. If it turns you on, you will do well in it. If you understand business, you will do well in investing.

Under-spend your income – save first.

American Express, Gillette, and Coke have businesses abroad.

Charitable foundation - gives away 5% of holdings per year.

One person died - sold 250 million dollars of Berkshire - no effect on our stock price.

Question: Is Buffettology true?

Warren: Not exactly. No quarrel with it though.

Read our reports. Get it better. Larry did a good job on annual reports. Better read.

Question: Why did you sell Disney in 60s?

Warren: Mistake. Don't worry about it.

Post mortem on capital expenditure is good.

Question: Will the end of U.S.S.R. change things?

Warren: No. Coke and Gillette helped by this. Coke and Gillette will grow faster out of the U.S., than in the U.S.

I won't tell Nebraska Furniture Mart to take American Express charge card.

Question: Do you believe in Inheritance?

Warren: Would like none. Leave enough to do anything, not enough to do nothing.

We (Charlie and I) are wired to be good at capital allocation.

Charlie: I see few people ruined by money. They would have been ruined anyway.

Question: Which is better BRKA or BRKB?

Warren: A or B is ok. We never recommend buy or sell.

U.S. stock market is not overvalued - if interest rates stay low and corporate profits stay up.

Every $1 retained has produced more than $1 in market value.

BRK Market price has tracked intrinsic value pretty well.

Question: Do you plan to split class A?

Warren: No.

Question: What about Japan?

Warren: Earning less.

Future earnings determine value.

Low price to book means nothing to us.

Don't like airlines. USAir $50 per share down to $4 per share. Lent them money with conversion privilege.

Would lend to those we would not buy.

Corporate tax cut in Japan would help - corporate culture in a foreign country is difficult to judge.

Hate correlation coefficient.

We don't pay any attention to Beta. The focus is 10 years from now.

Depreciation equals approximate capital required.

Adding capital to See's doesn't help.

Flight Safety--it does.

Coke--it does overseas.

Question: What is the difference between good business and bad business?

Warren: A good business keeps throwing up easy decisions. A bad business—they are all tough decisions.

I was on the Coke Board for 10 years - all easy decisions; USAir Board - all hard.

Don't expect depression or bear market. But would benefit from severe bear markets.

Over 20 years well prepared. We will not sell all and go to cash and wait for bear market.

Question: Person wanted advice on Berkshire Hathaway Stock.

Warren: No advice on Berkshire Hathaway stock.

Question: How long wait to buy?

Answer: Long time.

Occasional dull stretch – no problem.

Real estate has been bad.

Charlie: We lost on a tract in L.A. because the zoning authority was taking advantage of us.

Warren: I tried to buy a town at age 21 in Ohio.

Sell old plant - bad - should have.

TOB suit = Mad Hatters Tea Party.

Credit to Volker.

Scuttlebutt - don't do much now because already did it.

But it is good to talk to competitors.

Question: What competitor do you fear the most?

Warren: Andy Grove - silver bullet.

Frank at Hertz gave great insight.

Earnings lower? Mean nothing. Look through (earnings) grow at a reasonable rate. Gain in intrinsic value per share.

The industry that cash is earned in means nothing. It all spends the same.

Use same discount rate for all.

Business as taught at Wharton (Business School) is nonsense.

Charlie: Business school teaching volatility in corporate finance is nonsense.

Warren: Volatility is good.

Buy and sell McDonald's – good business.

We want shareholders like us. Trustee capitalism - not faceless nothings.

Quality vs price.

How would I feel if I own forever – not 3-5 years?

Comfortable price based on interest rates.

Last year trimmed certain holdings.

The trick is to get more in quality than you pay in price.

Question: Tax free spinoffs to shareholders?

Warren: No interest.

Borsheim's operating cost is less than most, including Tiffany's. It could be good on internet; also, GEICO. Anything that is a good deal (to the consumer) has internet possibility.

McDonald's owns 1/3 of its locations worldwide. Dairy Queen has 6,000 operations and only 30 owned by the company. Much less investment in fixed assets. Both depend on success of franchisee. Four percent fee is low charge to franchisee.

I agree with Milton Freidman; fix education in the U.S.

Charlie: Go to vouchers.

Warren: Need good public school system.

Look for honesty. Need some evidence - if you work with them for a few months, you know. Solomon separated them out. Leave lunch money on their desk. Don't take credit for things don't do. Give credit to your people. Leave track records.

Year 2000--no problem.

McDonald's 23,000 locations.

Charlie: Net returns on capital are high.

Warren: Double taxation.

Coke $1.2 billion cost – market value is $15 billion.

Tax again through BRK.

Ok because don't sell.

No cure for corporate income tax.

Acquisition due diligence = boilerplate – bad.

Deal is usually our guess of future economics of the business.

Business economics is 95% of deal-making.

The meeting ends at 3:00 p.m.

After The Meeting:
There are several other fun activities that happen on the weekend of the Berkshire Hathaway Shareholders Meeting in Omaha.

In 1998, on the Friday before the meeting, Warren sat at a table behind Dairy Queen at 114th and Dodge, and you could wait in line and then sit with him, shake his hand, get his autograph, and have your picture taken with him.

Now, on the Friday night prior to the meeting, there is a huge cocktail party at Borsheim's Jewelry Store at 108th and Dodge Streets. Thousands of shareholders mingle, look at and purchase expensive, as well as inexpensive jewelry, vases, figurines, ornaments, etc. They also serve complementary roast beef sandwiches, coke, wine and mixed drinks. There is an ice sculpture bar in a tent outside of the store where food and drinks are served, and live music plays. For the past few years, Grey Goose has sculpted the bar and served its own complementary vodka drinks.

On meeting day, there is a shareholder tour of Net Jets (a Berkshire Company) in a hangar at the Omaha Airport. There are different sizes of Net Jets for the shareholders to tour, and timeshare-type purchases may be made.

On the Sunday after the meeting, there is another party at Borsheim's, where more complementary food and beverages are served. In addition, these days, Warren and Bill Gates play bridge in an open mall area, with various stockholders. One year, they played ping pong with an 11- year old Chinese girl who wants to represent the U.S. in the Olympics some day.

On Sunday night, if you have reservations, you can have

dinner at Warren's favorite restaurant, Gorat's. And, we hear, he is always on hand to eat his favorite steak during this event. If you plan to do this, it is necessary to make your reservations well in advance. We don't attend this event, as our favorite steakhouse is Anthony's—which we always go to at least twice while we are in Omaha for the convention.

Chapter 2

In May, 1999, 10,000 shareholders attended the convention in Omaha, Nebraska at Ak-Sar-Ben.

Warren: We will be here to answer questions for 6 hours-- or until the candy runs out.

After a quick meeting to elect Berkshire Hathaway Board members, Warren asks, tongue-in cheek, whether Joe Stalin was ever any better.

Warren: A lot of people will say they are from Nebraska for status reasons.

We don't look at the market. We look at individual businesses.

We only buy value.

Money piles up; then we pile in.

We are the Geezer and the Geyser.

Gen Re - float. Cologne Re - 83% owned. Important incremental value. $24 Billion in float at Gen Re. Growth of float slow at Gen Re vs GEICO. $14 billion float, $6 billion premium.

Hedge fund - Long Term Capital – we were looking into bid for Long Term Capital Management. If we were in New York, we might have had the bid accepted. We made a firm bid from China for $100 billion in assets, $1 trillion in derivatives. Long-Term Capital did not accept. Fed arranged take over.

A report said the first hedge fund was in '49. Wrong. Ben Graham had a hedge fund in the '20s. Twenty percent participate in profits. My fund was a hedge fund. Charlie had one from '63 to '70s. They are enticing to money managers. You will see hundreds and hundreds of them.

You only have to get rich once. Don't risk losing it.

If a rich person goes broke, it usually includes borrowing (leverage).

Risk arbitrage we have been in for 40 years.

Accounting is weak. Clearing is weak.

Calculation of look-through earnings with discount rate.

Success in investing – retained earnings and float determine success.

Charlie: It is not a problem to have a pile of money.

Question: Retail? Internet retail?

Warren: Internet will have a huge impact on retail.

What will the business look like in 10 to 15 years?

Some retail we think threatened – not furniture.

Internet will be huge in many areas.

Borsheim's.com

Brand names will be big.

Tiffany - Borsheim's sells cheaper.

GEICO will benefit from the Internet.

Internet will affect real estate.

Retail progression – downtown - then mall - then Internet.

Alice Schroeder analysis of Berkshire.

Took kit – float based.

First-class analyst.

First comprehensive report.

One hundred billion market value - she understood insurance business. Good tool kit. $97,000 value.

Employee compensation – performance based; not option plan.

We have no PR department.

Don't cross-fertilize. No executive jumping.

Cheap float is best for us.

If our money wasn't there, we would borrow moderate amounts.

If only $1 million to invest, would use 50% compounding.

Greater amount of money, lower rate of compounding.

Leave the treasure hunt to us.

Charlie: It is harder now.

Warren: Could take $1 million and compound at 50% rate.

Stock options – corrupt accounting. Corporate America is hooked on it.

Should reflect cost of capital.

Disband business? No. They can get out.

'69 same market. No good buys.

Big expectations for 13 years.

No internal pressure here today.

'69 –'73 long time until it got back in.

There are waves of optimism and pessimism.

Talking to people now.

Question: Music video?

Warren: Like all kinds of music.

My two sisters are here today – I was on the radio in 1942 with them singing America the Beautiful.

Question: Communications buy? AT&T buy?

Warren: AT&T has been dismal the last 10 years.

I drive to Nebraska football games with Walter Scott (of Peter Kiewit & Sons).

There is a lot of difference between finding a good industry and making money in it.

1905-autos and airplanes.

Question: Would you want to come back as Warren Buffett?

Warren: Probably want to be Mrs. B (of Nebraska Furniture Mart).

Was a lot of fun. Does what he likes to do.

Charlie: We want to play our own games.

Question: How do you account for Goodwill?

Warren: Treat acquisition as purchase. Pay for goodwill – don't amortize.

Most of our businesses have increasing goodwill.

Make it an asset.

Australia has "cowboy" accounting.

White knight? Save companies from hostile takeovers? We want good companies.

Question: What about China--20% growth; 5 times earnings? Interested?

Warren: Could be.

Look at your area of expertise. We don't like to nibble. We want to take big gulps.

We always wanted to buy good companies.

You don't get as good of a buy in a large negotiated deal as you do if you buy stock in a firm. In the next five years, we will do both.

Question: Define rich vs wealthy. Don't want to sound like Clinton.

Warren: Rich – lot of money. Wealthy – healthy.

Money makes little difference after a certain amount.

My life is similar to a college student (except travel).

Charlie: What good is health? You can't buy money with it.

Warren: Work – important thing is who you do it with.

Question: What do you think about Pharmaceuticals?

Warren: If we could buy them at below market, we would. Could have in '93. Blew it.

Charlie: Large profits in drugs is good for us.

Question: Did you have to buy one share of every company to get each annual report?

Warren: Yes, I did. Now I buy 100 shares with the foundation – 200 companies. If you hold the stock in your own name, you get the information faster.

$500 million is our minimum investment now.

Coke - 35 times earnings. 5.8 billion people. Ten-20 years, Coke will go up.

Share of market –Share of mind. Good feeling about product.

Coke – unit-cases-sold keeps going up.

PE ratio now is unimportant if looking at 10 to 15 years out.

Hard to think of a much more solid industry.

Question: What do you think about Y2K?

Warren: – Don't think it will be a big deal.

Charlie: I mean it <u>was</u> predictable that it would happen.

Question: Is Japan a problem?

Warren: No factor in our thinking.

Charlie: Problem is the Japanese accounting system.

Question: Analyst coverage?

Warren: Don't care.

140 planes 1.5 billion – 7 billion dollars of planes on order.

Gen Re float.

Inflation and technology.

U.S. leads world in information technology.

Charlie: Steel-toed boots will not be obsolete.

Warren: Change to make money is not our idea of good.

Want stable in 10 – 15 years.

Coke is the same now as it was 50 years ago.

Invest in a low cost index fund – **keep investing on a regular basis.**

New York has more lawyers than people.

Can't average 15% in equities.

Investor makes what business makes.

All stocks – $334 billion profit, $10.5 trillion cost – GDP grow 4%.

Charlie: If a thing can't go on forever, it will eventually stop.

Warren: We paid $2.6 billion to federal government in taxes – more than GE or Microsoft. They have three times the market cap.

Question: What do you think about charity?

Warren: Not a big believer in giving away your money.

Deliver goods and services at low cost.

Cable Television business – Washington Post – we own 17%, 700,000 homes.

Question: Buy Omega REIT?

Warren: No, wrong press account.

Cable profits not that great. Programming – big profits.

What do you think about inheriting?

Warren: Not big on it.

Question: Why not buy high tech like Microsoft?

Warren: Don't see it as clear as Coke.

Would bet on Gates.

Willing to trade big payoff for certain payoff.

The Dilly Bar is more certain.

400 companies in U.S. earn $200 million after taxes – five years from now 450 – 475; 20 will come from nowhere; dozens selling at that rate, but won't make it.

Need market cap of 3 billion.

Question: Coke is down 30 – 50% from highs. When buy?

Warren: Dance in and out – bad idea. Best thing stick with it; Coke, Gillette, Cap Cities.

Blade razor business is great.

Deflation very unlikely, but can't predict; but actually good for investors – value of $ increase – lucky.

Business school – the market is fairly efficient, but that does not suffice to support efficient market theory – popular in academic world – required to hold a teaching position. It has been discredited. Seems less regarded now.

Florida and Missouri have value course.

Investment is about valuing a business. Can't find a course on it. Ben Graham did.

If you take a PHD in Finance and ask him to value a business, he is in trouble. They would calculate beta or something.

Float - 1967 to now – it grew at a faster rate than we thought it would.

Goal is to grow float fast with low cost.

Growth in intrinsic value of Berkshire will be affected by growth of float.

Question: What do you think about the Life Insurance business?

Warren: We have no bias against it, but it is not very profitable.

Also includes investment management – we are not interested in that.

We want the best ideas to go to Berkshire.

We have annuities for sale on our web site.

Shorting does not bother us.

Question: How can I make $30 billion?

Warren: Start young--or live to be old. Start with the A's in Moody's. Do your own research. Look for undervalued stocks. Learn what you know and what you don't know. Don't look for consensus. The first look is the hardest. Be rational. Underspend your income.

Don't need seat cushions at the meeting.

Web site reference documents.

Lorimar Davidson, GEICO.

I got an education reading annual reports.

Loss Cologne RE - $275 million.

Charlie: A dumb mistake refreshes your attention.

Question: Would you consider repurchasing Shares?

Warren: 1974 - $50 per share vs Washington Post; $80 million vs $400 million. We usually find something even more **underpriced,** but we would do it if it were dramatically underpriced.

Question: Have you considered Berkshire branding on internet?

Warren: Can do more – already do a lot of direct-to- customer business.

Use treasury rate to get - compare discount rate.

Management degree of certainty with business; it is an art.

Chewing gum unit - growth price elasticity.

Question: Is management bright or stupid?

Warren: Big moat – need less management. Have to understand business.

Charlie: You are not sufficiently critical of academics doing standard deviation.

We have done fewer dumb things.

Liberal arts teaches one to feel like a victim.

Question: Explain BRKA and BRKB.

Warren: One BRKA always equals 30 BRKB's. Does not convert the other way.

B periodically goes to a discount. B greater than 2 percent discount – buy B.

Insurance trends – consolidation, demutualization.

Winners – Good franchise, management, distribution system, float.

Coke – huge potential in China.

Fastest growth – Gillette - All shaving - How upgrade shaving experience. I would hate to compete against them. They have the winning hand.

Emerging market funds equals nonsense.

Sectors - same nonsense.

Charlie: Our game is to find a few intelligent things to do.

Hagstrom - *Buffett Portfolio* is great – has investing process. First book bad.

Like *J.D. Rockefeller Biography, Guns, Germs and Steel, The Wealth and Power of Nations.* Tobacco threat - serious more than drugs.

Warren: *Katharine Graham autobiography.*

Question: Kleiner Perkins Venture Capital – Why don't you do? Internet is the most important thing in the last 500 years.

Warren: **Early investment and promotion we understand. Internet VC funding – we have no interest. We will not turn your money over to someone else to manage.**

Question: Invest in high tech VC?

Warren: Call Bill Gates.

McDonald's – it was a mistake to sell. I cost you one billion dollars. We believe in post mortems.

Health insurance – Charlie runs a hospital. We don't know anybody to get in with.

Accounting and finance – go to the library; take out every book. Learn from great business magazines. You need a massive amount of reading.

Go away for 10 years - put your money in one company - which one? Bill Gates said Coke.

Do journalistic investigation; ask competitors.

Charlie: Value Line – what is the chart going to look like in the next 10 years? Keep asking why.

Question: How does Berkshire add value to companies?

Warren: Float, tax advantages, move faster.

Executive Jet got on the map faster because it was associated with Berkshire.

We enable managers to spend more time on what they do best.

CEO publishing company wastes 13% of his time on non-productive things.

We have no board meetings.

In many companies there is a large group of people whose importance is measured by meddling in the affairs of the people doing the work.

Stocks – intrinsic value – use market value.

Chapter 3

Eleven thousand shareholders attended the April 29, 2000, Berkshire Hathaway Stockholder Meeting in the Civic Auditorium at 29th & Capitol in downtown Omaha, Nebraska. The Auditorium was once a basketball arena, with an exhibit hall below. This is the year that lots of Berkshire-owned companies began exhibiting their goods at the convention. This proved to add a lot of fun to the event.

Warren: Growth and value are not distinct.

The amount of cash you have at judgment day = worth.

There is no distinction between growth and value in our minds.

Buy value - expect growth - very simple!

The first primer was 600 BC from Aesop – A bird in the hand is worth two in the bush.

Think like you are buying the whole company.

$500 billion 10% rate of return; 55 billion next year; or 60.5 year 3 in perpetuity - disgorge to you. $80 billion per year pre tax.

Charlie: All intelligent investing is value investing.

Warren: High tech stocks - possible fall out.

The amount of cash a stock can disgorge = price or worth.

Stock goes up with no cash – no wealth created – just wealth transfer.

The stock market is a voting machine.

Twenty years ago – there was farmland mania.

Momentum investing goes on for a long time, but not forever.

Charlie: Wretched excess = wretched consequences.

The opportunity to monetize shareholder ignorance has never been greater.

Question: Has the Internet hurt your company?

Warren: No religious belief. We don't buy tech companies. We just don't know one that we know what it will look like in 10 years.

We should think about how it affects our business.

Washington Post and Buffalo News - We talk about how to use the internet.

Newspapers are threatened by the Internet.

Charlie: Afraid of the Internet? Yes.

Warren: No magic in one-year periods. We will have down years. We have had a down ½ year.

Our capital allocation job in '99 was poor.

Coke and Gillette - bad years. High market share. World market share - 50% Coke - 70% Gillette.

It will gain share over time. Coke: sells 1 billion 8-ounce servings per-day. Berkshire owns 8% of Coke, 6% of Gillette.

Charlie: Own marketable securities in excess of its net worth.

Question: Business risk?

Warren: Ask what can happen 5, 10, or 15 years from now to hurt your business?

We are risk adverse. We are not against losing $1 billion on an earthquake if the math is ok.

If too much could go wrong, we forget it.

Is the moat around the castle subject to marauders?

Sees candy has a good moat.

We want to widen the moat every year.

If tenuous, too risky, we stay away.

Gen Re uncovers it was a mistake – reserve $275 million.

One in the '70's - cost us $4 million--which would equate to $8 or $9 billion today.

Guy writing bonds on your paper.

National Indemnity, Gen Re have terrific records over time.

Insurance will have surprises, but will be good.

Last week we bought another one (insurance company).

GEICO - great company! A mistake in the '70s almost broke the company, but it helped us.

Insurance is attractive for fraud. You hand them (the customer) a piece of paper; they give you money.

No guarantee of principal.

Problem of a wonderful business is the temptation to get into a not so wonderful business.

Share of mind becomes share of market.

American Express name = huge value.

We bought GEICO when it was losing money.

We don't have a set PE ratio for buy - no buy.

We want a great stream of cash estimate over 10 or 20 years.

Question: Are you going to buy Tech?

Warren: We will not buy anything we don't understand.

36

We do not look at the stock price and feel poor or rich. We look at the business and feel richer or poorer.

Question: BRK vs dollar and interest rates?

Warren: We don't know what they (interest rates) are going to do. If we did, we would just invest in those.

The stock price will eventually follow the value of the company.

Focus on what is knowable and important.

The best time to buy stocks was when interest rates were high.

Holdings – M&T Bank - added a good bank. Disney ownership fell below threshold (to report). We still own some.

We would like to buy businesses, not equities right now.

Charlie: Read Fortune article.

Question: Will Berkshire ever pay a dividend?

Warren: In 1969, we paid $.10 per share. **We would do a large dividend**--or none at all. We will keep it (retained earnings) if we can make more on it than if give it away.

We will do no spin-offs.

We want a rational compensation plan.

$90 billion market value - Berkshire.

We have had great success keeping managers.

Charlie: Free medical care forever is stupid.

Warren: Stock options = lottery tickets.

Look through book value would not mean much.

Now businesses are worth more than book value.

The market can get crazy.

Don't see great under value any place right now.

We would love to find a business to buy that is selling for ½ what it is worth.

Today – to monetize shareholder ignorance has never been easier.

Buffalo News will do as well as the top 50 Internet companies.

Easy to copy.

Street car tracks.

Idiot nephew.

Insurance is a commodity business. Average will not cut it. Insurance will be good.

Charlie: Some businesses die - like stamps. We wring money out of them, and then go elsewhere.

Warren, Porter at Harvard – have not read, but we think alike.

Durable competitive advantage is more important than P&L

study.

Copy people that have been successful like Gillette, Mrs. B.

A new See's Barbie doll is being introduced here today.

Cost of options should be in the Annual Report.

U.S. 10 year life - make educated guess what they are going to do. How much they could have sold for on the open market. Taking 1/3 of cost is probable. You see a lot of repricing of options - option schemes.

Leave out raises.

Options subtract value.

Warren visits MBA schools.

Moody's moat is better than operating company.

Great teacher Ben Graham of Columbia University.

Question: What do you think about investing in an Energy company?

Warren: Maybe.

Question: Transportation?

Warren: No. Bad investment.

Question: What about Ivestor (of Coke) severance policy?

Warren: He was an asset to the company. Ivestor was a good CFO – he was not right for CEO. He was Roberto's hand-picked successor.

Charlie: Stupid. He was sold stuff by consultants.

Warren: CEO shows up with 20-page contract and a lawyer.

Institutional shareholders own top 30 companies. They do not seem to care.

Question: What do you think about Deflation?

Warren: Don't know - probably not. Don't get into macro factors.

Having an economics department at a bank is dumb.

Role model is good.

Early model is parent.

Charlie: The eminent dead.

Question: Would you take Greenspan's job?

Warren: No.

Charlie: No.

Warren: We don't want public sector jobs. **We love our jobs!**

Question: How do you pick managers?

Warren: I think I can do it well, but I cannot come up with a list of questions.

Do they love the business or love the money?

Metropolitan Museum of Businesses.

If you love your business, it means something to you.

Charlie: Andrew Carnegie, Ben Franklin.

Warren: Our businesses have standards.

To hire an investment banker to evaluate businesses to buy is idiocy. If we cannot evaluate it, we are in trouble.

Question: Do you understand Tech stocks?

Warren: We understand them – we just don't know where they will be 10 years from now.

Bill Gates (Microsoft) and Andy Grove (Intel) would say the same thing.

Question: What will happen to Berkshire if you are hit by a truck?

Warren: My estate is in BRK, so I am confident.

Question: Do you want to buy the Omaha World Herald?

Warren: No.

Question: Cost of float vs Internet?

Warren: It will not increase the cost of float.

I always look at the economics of a business.

The internet is good for society - bad for capitalists. It will reduce the profitability of American businesses.

Charlie: Perfectly obvious, so little understood.

Warren: So there! Knight, Castle, Moat!

Compensation committee - nobody wants to be in the lower half of compensation. It can only go up. I have been on 19 corporate boards.

Last compensation committee – Solomon.

Some behave well.

It is mostly ego.

I don't like to see .270 hitter getting more than me. I am a .400 hitter.

You can only belch so many times at the dinner table and be invited back.

More goods and services per-capita will mean more money available to take care of old people.

Best Warren Buffett book is the Larry Cunningham book – 20 Years of Annual Reports - on Internet – better than these books. They add formulas – it is not there really.

Charlie: What we did is not hard to do. Not hard to get (understand). Many don't get it.

Warren: Purchase of Berkshire Hathaway was a terrible mistake – cigar butt – $7.50 per share - 2000 shares. I thought I would be offered $10-$12 - maybe then sell.

Stanton (of Berkshire) asks tender price? I said 11-3/8. He came in 1/8 lower which irritated me, so I bought more and more.

Similar Blue Chip – stumbled into. Berkshire just went along – wrong base to use – made it fun.

Charlie: Interesting that the wrong decision worked out. Big part of life – turn lemons into lemonade.

Warren: We started with three disasters - Berkshire, Diversified, and Blue Chip.

Question: Exchange for gold coins?

Warren: Never. Some piece of metal - dig out of ground in Africa – transport - store at Ft. Knox. Producing asset vs non-producing asset.

People love predictions, but they are just space fillers in newspapers. Know 7.0 earthquake in California in the next 50 years.

Charlie: Jew in Vienna in 1939, maybe (gold would be good for).

Question: Is anybody dumb enough to sell back to you under $45,000?

Warren: No.

Question: Does Float add increased value?

Warren: We add at different layers of cost. Cost of float and growth of float.

Charlie: I am amazed at how well we have done on generating float.

Warren: It is competitive. Others try to copy.

We will find a few things to do.

Question: WESCO vs intrinsic value (in Freddie Mac).

Charlie: We pay no attention to the price of WESCO stock.

Question: What is the succession in Berkshire Hathaway?

Warren: Making me useless, so I won't be missed.

Question: EVA?

Charlie: A lot of twaddle and bullshit. In EVA turn retained money into more EVA - has cost of capital. Ideas that make no sense. Mental system as a whole does not work.

Question: What is your relationship with Bill Gates?

Warren: I cannot speak for Bill. Met him - Meg Greenfield of Washington Post, loved state of Washington – living in D.C. – she asked me if she could afford a second home in Washington state. I said "yes." She bought a home in Washington in 1991. I visited on July 4 (she was a friend of Bill's parents). Bill did not want to come to the party, but did to meet Kate Graham. We hit it off. We play bridge and golf together. He is very competitive.

Charlie: Sympathetic to Microsoft case.

Warren: On case - 20 years ago inferiority complex – Japan and Germany eating our lunch. Then technology. We swept the world aside. Can't see who is in second place. Don't tinker with it or go in with a meat axe. We know it is a huge benefit to society.

Charlie: Big picture lost--radios, TVs. Huge lead in software.

Somebody drawing a salary from U.S. Government wants to destroy it?

Warren: Insurance is a low-cost producer over time. **Compared to an e-retailer, Insurance is far superior.**

GEICO - Tony – I have known him for years. I have never heard him say anything that did not make sense.

Question: What about Mid-American Energy?

Warren: Embedded cost of generation. David Sokol can generate good ideas.

Question: Float vs Claim $?

Warren: Use float for anything we want--float plus other streams of income. Try to get liability low – employ assets high. Don't match up assets to future liabilities.

Lou Simpson of GEICO – $2 billion in float – makes own decisions on stocks

Jones apparel – good

Liz – someone offered it to us at a good price and we bought it – decent record

Question: What about Freddie Mac?

Warren: Too much political undertones.

Want active successor - not caretaker.

Insurance is a large part of the budget of most people in the country. Cost of an average policy is $40 - $1,100.

Teaching in universities is bad.

We like good businesses with potential to expand. International market. Some travel well; some don't. Candy bars don't. Dr. Pepper: 18% Texas - .6% Boston. Geographic expansion is not as easy as it looks.

Wrote a letter to a guy in Germany. He hasn't written back.

Want $3 or $4 per $1 lay down – not $.90 – will take $1.10.

We will spend money to expand GEICO and NetJets in Europe.

Question: Why were the Annual Reports late?

Warren: Registered holder will get it two days after it is on the Internet. Street-names holder is 9 of 10 - Designated mailer slow, who is designated by your broker.

Sustainable competitive advantage – GEICO – low cost producer – good service. Not in MA or NJ. Have to distinguish good or bad drivers.

Costco is big on low cost.

Internet - important to GEICO. Click to compare. Must be low cost.

Real estate financing over $100 million – three deals last two years – will do if find good opportunity. No department for this. Like Tiger fund? No. Thirty years ago closer than now. We own businesses; generate capital; buy some stocks.

Charlie: Relative performance game; they try to attract hot money.

Warren: Intelligence - honesty; we only look for those types of companies.

If organization lies at the top, employees adopt that as their policy, too.

We do not try to reform companies.

Question: What about Reinsurance?

Warren: We have been in this business for 30 years.

No volume goals at Berkshire or Gen Re. So we don't write insurance too cheap.

Chapter 4

Nineteen thousand shareholders attended the May 1, 2004, Berkshire Hathaway Stockholder meeting at the Qwest Center, Omaha, Nebraska.

At that time, the Quest Center was the new convention center facility. It was built at 10th and Capitol in downtown Omaha. Quest has a basketball arena that holds about 19,000 people, and a large attached exhibit hall north of the arena.

This year, the Berkshire exhibitors had expanded exponentially. Firms like GEICO, Coca Cola, Sees Candy, Dairy Queen, Fruit of the Loom, Nebraska Furniture Mart, Mid-American Energy, Justin Boots, Net Jets, and Pampered Chef were doing booming business inside the Exhibit Hall. Everywhere we looked, people were carrying their purchases inside sacks emblazoned with each company's logo.

The shareholder meeting was held in the basketball arena. It was then, and continues to be jam-packed to the rafters by 7:30 a.m. In the afternoon, there are some empty seats, but don't count on it. There are large TVs in the Exhibit Hall broadcasting the meeting, so you can shop and watch the meeting at the same time.

The movie before the meeting was hilarious. In one segment, Arnold Schwarzenegger had to drop Warren from his campaign (Warren wanted to do away with Prop 13 [a low property tax bill]; there was also a Terminator cartoon spoof on the "Warrenator" and the "Charlinator" coming back from the future. Susie (Warren's wife) sang a song to the tune of "The Real Thing," but with words describing all the Berkshire CEOs. It was a really big hit!

Warren: He said he was working on Liberty Kids Video.

He said he was going to leave the board of Coke.

We like shareholders to behave like owners - not sheep – can behave like intelligent owners.

Check lists are bad.

Directors select manager.

We have $10 billion at Coke in stock.

Inflation. Have earning power of your own. Own businesses that can price in inflationary terms.

Don't require capital - like See's.

Inflation is the enemy of the investor.

Inflation adjusted bonds.

We don't like meetings with institutional investors or have questions for managers.

Charlie: **Don't talk to analysts.**

Warren: We are not about enticing new shareholders.

It is a waste of our managers' time to talk to analysts.

We have $130 billion market cap. We don't need to talk about small parts.

Warren said "I tell Charlie I'm thinking of buying a stock" and he says, "It's not your worst idea." That is high praise from Charlie.

Question: What about compensation?

Warren: Related to performance.

Mid-American - I did in three minutes.

No one formula – short one or two paragraphs.

We have no compensation consultant.

We have no HR department.

We have no Investors' Relations Committee.

Question: Investments?

Warren: High grade bonds; junk bonds, arbitrage, etc.

Question: What is best for Berkshire money?

Warren: Some we understand – some not.

In '02, junk bonds looked good - then that ended.

We don't prioritize categories.

Arbitrage is not too good right now.

Charlie: We don't think about an order of precedence.

Warren: Buy junk bonds like common stocks - was 40% yield-
-now 6% yield – company worth?

Present value discount formula.

St. Petersburg Paradox by Durant.

High growth rate 9% vs 7% discount rate.

Question: Stock Exchange Specialists?

Charlie: The system has worked pretty well.

Warren: Charlie had a specialist firm. 13 years GM on Pacific
Stock Exchange.

Question: What about Derivatives?

Warren: Probability not high for trauma, but there.

Freddie Mac - plus oversight committees - auditor - misstate
earnings by $6 billion – partly derivatives.

In '91, we prepared bankruptcy papers at Solomon if the
Treasury Department ruled wrong.

Use some time in the future.

There will be some problems.

Charlie: Consequences of consequences.

Warren: They used derivatives to smooth out lumpiness at Solomon.

Charlie: Bonkers and the accountants sold out.

Warren: They argued derivatives will spread the risk.

Bill Gates is the smartest person. He can do your job – not you his.

Question: Will Bill Gates become Chairman of Berkshire by merger or he resign Microsoft and come to Berkshire?

Warren: **Did Bill put you up to this?** (Big Laugh from the audience.)

We have four people in Berkshire that can do my job.

Fifteen years ago, we did not have four.

I like the culture at Berkshire – like the person inside.

Question: Do you have any reading recommendations?

Warren: When young, look at company you understand. Read everything in sight on business and its industry.

Charlie: We read a lot and thought a lot. Also need temperament to grab good ideas.

Warren: Money mind – **temperament is all important.**

It does not require extended intellect, but extended discipline.

Charlie: _Deep Simplicity_ book.

Warren, *A Short History of Nearly Everything*.

Newton – Lead Into Gold.

He lost money in the South Seas Bubble.

Question: What about taxes?

Warren: Pam Olsen – I owe her an apology. She stopped some tax shelters.

Middle class pays too much tax.

If 540 companies pay what we do in taxes, no others would have to pay taxes.

Charlie: Accounting firms selling fraudulent tax shelters.

Question: What about Math?

Charlie: To understand science, you need math.

For business, you don't need high math.

Warren: My mother sang me songs about compound interest rates.

Question: What about mistakes?

Warren: We did not invest or did not maximize.

Charlie: Wal-Mart.

Warren: $10 billion; bought some; it went up; thumb-sucking.

We will make mistakes.

Charlie: We rub our noses in our mistakes.

Question: What Mutual Fund should I Invest with?

Charlie: Hunt.

Warren: Won't find many.

Warren: If you find one, go big. To diversify is wrong.

Advisors is a tough one. In 1969, recommended two people - Sandy and Bill.

Don't know any now.

Promotional-type not good.

Some loaded up on Berkshire years ago.

Charlie: Difficult. Some mutual fund managers took bribes to defraud fund holders.

Warren: Many already rich. I think others knew of it. Hundreds of people.

Question: What about Asset Allocation Models?

Warren: Minimize risk by thinking 60-40 to 65-35 is **nonsense.**

Instead find something; do it.

Asset Allocation is merchandising. You don't need them.

Charlie: People always wanted to know the future. Always a market for this.

Workers compensation fraud by carriers on manufacturers.

Warren: Plenty of fraud in Insurance. Lost a lot of money - Workers Compensation.

6.0 earthquake in California last 50 years – 26 – assume 32 – say premium $1 million, then had margin of safety; not difficult.

Charlie: That book used Power Law Formula.

Warren: A 9.0 earthquake is harder to value.

You don't have to do hard stuff in investing.

Question: Does Government shape moats?

Warren: Varies in different businesses – regulation big in Energy and Insurance.

Charlie: In the early days, we overestimated regulations; like, we did not buy TV stations because of it.

Question: Should I buy S&P 500 Index Fund or BRK?

Warren: I don't say to buy Berkshire. If you buy an Index Fund, over 10 years, you will do well.

Charlie: Index fund - do good.

Question: What if there is a catastrophic event in next 50 years?

Warren: We think about it – so **we don't do a lot of leverage.**

It is the one thing that can keep you from playing out your hand.

You want to be able to ride it out.

Question: What about Enron?

Warren: You pick up signals.

Options should be expensed.

Google Indiana and Pi. Indiana legislature changed the value of Pi to 3.20.

Question: Why don't you manage a mutual fund?

Warren: Too hard. Ethical problems. It has been put to us, but we don't want to do it.

Question: Buy companies?

Warren: We don't buy them cheap.

Stocks sometimes are cheap.

We would rather buy businesses than stocks.

Need a big business.

Committee for social responsibility? David Sokol of Mid American, I was a ranger in President Bush's election.

Question: What do you think about good immigration?

Charlie: I would like talented people to come in; not the bottom of the mental barrel.

Question: What do you think about Stock splits?

Warren: We like more long-term investors – low turnover.

Charlie: Liquidity is good is "twaddle." Berkshire trades 50 million per day.

Question: What about ethical decisions in asset allocation?

Warren: I drink five cokes a day. I will buy stock in a company, but may not buy the whole company (like a tobacco company).

Question: Is there an incentive to not underwrite bad business?

Warren: We don't have a culture of writing bad Insurance business. No layoffs.

Charlie: Nobody else does it.

Controlling shareholder with strong opinions.

Question: Why invest in Petro China?

Warren: The company is not complicated

They produce 85% as much crude oil as Exxon.

Their annual report is good.

They pay out 45% of their earnings in dividends.

We bought it because it was very, very cheap.

Question: What about Tort reform?

Charlie: Is Mesothelioma lung cancer from asbestos or two-pack- a-day smokers?

Bought expert witness who says any spot on the lung is asbestos.

In all 50 states, jury pool hates big corporations.

No stopping it.

25% going to victims.

Supreme Court ducked it.

Congress could fix it, but won't.

Warren: We own Johns Manville. They went bankrupt. We bought them. No connection to old company. Manville personal injury trust paying out 5% of $2 billion on asbestos claims.

Question: What about Dividend vs Stock buy backs?

Warren: If you can buy stock below value - do it.

Some do it to keep stock from going down.

Dividend - don't bounce about.

Charlie: Trading cost equals amount spent on Dividend.

Warren: I did an article on frictional cost of trading stocks.

$30 billion of cash at Berkshire. If can't use, then repurchase stock or dividend.

Question: What about GEICO direct marketing?

Warren: Leo Goodwin - Government Employees – GEICO bypass agent – Progressive is competitor – GEICO is low-cost operation.

Dell is low-cost.

Charlie is a director at Costco.

The low-cost producer is a good bet.

Question: Is the Google Owner's Manual like Berkshire?

Warren: They said they were influenced by Berkshire.

Question: Are Mid-American real estate commissions sustainable?

Warren: Yes.

Internet is a threat to any business.

Phil Fisher died? Great man – in 90s, met once – it was in the books – him and Graham – met Charlie in '59.

Charlie: I like it when somebody attractive to me agrees with me.

Question: How is compensation for managers determined?

Warren: No formula. Return on equity? Assets.

Charlie: <u>Les Schwab Autobiography</u> is great on compensation.

Warren: Wal-Mart and Costco have good systems.

Question: Please discuss IPOs.

Charlie: Use our method for IPO - could yes, but **average person who buys an IPO gets creamed.**

Warren: Like a negotiated sale.

Question: What do you think Interest rates will do in future?

Warren: We are not worried about it.

American business has not let down American people. They have let themselves down.

Question: Derivatives Gen Re?

Warren: Gen Re derivatives were not like their Insurance; they were speculative.

Charlie: Collateral posting if credit goes down.

Warren: We fixed it.

Charlie: Solomon seeking the business of the bouncing check.

Question: What about Hedge Funds?

Warren: No - now a fad.

Charlie: Why? One-two-three layers of fees.

Warren: Good at marketing.

Question: Please discuss Value investing and habits?

Warren: Not always learning principle.

Learn more about business.

Temperament is most important.

Intrinsic value? Present value of cash in future.

1st Quarter? 10Q in a few days. No information.

No credit card debt.

Charlie, Stay away from evil women.

Question: What about the price of Silver?

Warren: The market is not rigged. Most that write on gold and silver have theories.

Question: What about Wells Fargo and derivatives?

Warren: Don't think it is a big position. It is a well-managed bank.

Question: If financial institutions collapse, how is Berkshire protected?

Warren: We are not worried about it.

Leverage is bad.

Berkshire is in a strong position with cash.

Cash and courage when the world was panicking.

Chapter 5

Twenty-two thousand shareholders attended the April 30, 2005 Berkshire Hathaway Shareholder meeting in the Qwest Center in Omaha, Nebraska.

In the Exhibit Hall before the meeting, we watched and listened to Warren playing his beloved ukulele, with the Fruit of the Loom Singing Fruit People. The song they played and sang was "Ain't She Sweet."

Prior to the movie, we noticed Warren walk up the aisle and take a seat in the audience to enjoy the pre-meeting movie. The movie was great. It featured a cartoon spoof on the "Wizard of Oz;" only this one was called the "Wizard of Omaha," with Warren as Dorothy, Arnold as the Lion, Bill Gates as the Scarecrow, Charlie as the Tin Man, and Alan Greenspan as the Wizard of Oz. The movie also had Arnold making Warren do push-ups and sit-ups in fast motion for daring to even mention Prop 13.

The movie also had a segment with Judge Judy hearing a case between Warren and Bill Gates over a $2 bridge bet, where Bill had unplugged his computer to avoid losing.

There was an All My Children Soap Opera segment with Erica, Warren, and Tom Murphy. There was also a tour of the newly remodeled "lavish" corporate office in the Kiewit Building.

Warren: No information on Gen Re investigation.

1st Quarter $500 million insurance.

GEICO: 245,000 new policies

We are a big writer of Cat (catastrophe) insurance.

Done in September.

September is the big-risk quarter for hurricanes.

We have $45 Billion in float – free money.

All Insurance did well.

Investments up $100 million.

Before tax, investment gain up $400 million.

We have $21 billion in investments.

$300 million loss.

Up and down $200 million-per-day.

We have to mark on the day at the end of the quarter.

If Procter and Gamble buys Gillette, $4 Billion Dollar gain for Berkshire – meaningless.

We won't earn at the rate of the 1st quarter throughout the year.

We will soon announce a $1 billion acquisition in the Insurance field.

We have $44 billion in cash.

We have more money than brains.

Question: What is your criteria for managers?

Warren: They have a passion for their business – avoid dampening it – **intelligence, energy, integrity – if they have no integrity, we want dumb and lazy – do they love the money or love the business?**

We have 16 employees at the Berkshire headquarters.

Charlie: It is amazing how well it works, and how few copy it.

Warren: Anheuser Busch--didn't talk about it – made the decision in two seconds – bought 100 shares 25 years ago.

Observe consumer habits – beer industry sales are flat.

Bud earnings are flat.

Spend money to maintain share.

Easy to understand product and consumer behavior.

Omaha was a brewing town. Storz had 50% of Omaha.

Beer not growing in U.S.

Worldwide - BIG.

Charlie: Need unpleasantness to buy in a large company.

Warren: Same in Berkshire.

Average person drinks 64 oz per day – 28% cola/10% beer/ 10% of all liquids – coffee down, down, down.

Question: Hedge fund?

Charlie: Three in small town.

Warren: No doubt more money looking at deals now than five years ago. Looking at good buy - mundane companies.

Pay up.

Private equity firms sell to other private equity firms. Near-term not good.

Ended partnership in 1969 because too much money.

Four years later, there were great opportunities.

1998 was the same--we bought $7 billion in junk bonds then.

Now positioned badly to buy business.

Charlie: Private Equity Funds buy fee motivated.

Warren: Some have 2% fee.

We go up and down in BRK, so only want to go up.

Sparked interest in investing – **got interested at age 7 – wasted my time before that.**

My dad was in the business – I would go to his office on the 4th floor at 17th and Farnam – Harris Upman was on the second floor

I read a lot – every book in the Omaha Public Library on the stock market.

At 11, I bought three shares of stock.

My dad was in Congress, so I got a bigger library.

I read the Graham book while at the University of Nebraska at age 19.

It is a huge advantage to start young in any field.

There are no secrets only the priesthood knows.

It requires temperament, not I.Q.

Develop a framework.

Look for opportunities that fit within it.

Don't act every day.

If you enjoy it, you will do well.

Charlie: Corporations should study investing to become better managers.

Warren: Managers do better if they understand investing.

Sodom and Gomorra – We weren't there.

Petro China – we bought it (stock) a few years ago.

$400 million.

They produce 3% of world's oil.

80% of Exxon Oil amount.

Market value was $35 million.

Annual report was in English.

They pay out 45% of their earnings in dividends.

Chinese government owns 90%.

We own 1.3%

It employs 500,000 people.

BP and Exxon Mobil only larger companies.

Only read their Annual Report before investing.

Paid $400 million; now it is worth $1.2 billion.

It was selling at a discount.

Price increase – carpet, etc. because of oil – lag on pass-through cost – use natural gas - Johns Manville, Acme Brick pass through.

Corporate profits are at an all-time high as a % of GDP – corporate taxes are at an all-time low.

We like to buy businesses with untapped pricing power – like See's Candy.

It is not a great business if you have to have a prayer session before raising prices.

Now newspapers have trouble raising prices. Thirty years ago, big yawn – did it anyway – now agonize over it.

Other media – you can learn a lot about the durability of a business by looking at price increases.

We have the best group of shareholders.

Dividend? 15% tax. We say if no tax, still same – retain $1 - earn more than $1 – 1% after tax then shift – then dividend a couple of years from now.

Trade deficit $618 billion – something will happen to change – some say soft landing – transfer wealth abroad

Electronic herd – some event could cause a stampede – can see bubbles develop – to predict what will happen is easier than when it will happen.

Charlie: I am repelled by the lack of virtue in the consumer credit and public finance system. Will stand a lot of abuse - how end? Bad.

Warren: If you sit on the porch - own a vast acreage – consume 6% more than you produce - sell off small % of farm or mortgage it to pay for it. If it goes on too long, we don't own it any more. In the U.S., we send out $2 billion per day.

Charlie: counter argument – What if foreigners own 2% of country if value goes up 30%.

Warren: Only $21 billion in foreign exchange contracts.

Declining housing or carpet? Make up elsewhere.

We are not big on Macro forecasts.

Buy a good business – selling at a cheap price.

Once cash is trash.

Buy farmland - sold for $2,000 per acre in 1980. I bought for $600 per acre from the FDIC.

Charlie: Housing bubble - L.A.

Warren: I sold a $3.5 million dollar house in Laguna Beach – $500,000 house – land $3 million – 2,000 square feet - .20 acre – $60 million per acre.

I heard a house sold for $27 million – a modest house with an ocean view. **At $27 million, I'd rather stare at my bathtub.**

Insurance – correlation of risk of earthquake in California – Twenty-five 6.0's in the last 25 years – National Indemnity, Gen Re.

We Don't own Freddie or Fannie now.

Most likely mega hurricane - 9.0 earthquake or Force 5 Hurricane - everything that can happen will happen.

They had an 8.0 earthquake in Missouri once.

We want to be prepared for the worst.

We exclude nuclear and biological.

We insure a large airport - $500 million - excess $2.5 billion - not nuclear or biological. Somebody pays $2.5 billion, and then we pay $500 million.

Insure final four against being cancelled – $75 million – same for Grammys.

Nuclear terrorism book - lastbestchance.org.

Charlie: We care about it more – 60-foot tidal wave in California.

Warren: We worry more about downside.

We don't borrow a lot of money.

Aunt Katie had all her money in Berkshire.

Education in America – I dedicated a school in Omaha named for Aunt Alice.

We have good schools in Omaha.

Good education takes the interest of parents and the well–to-do.

They should put more money towards teaching and less towards overhead and administration.

Number one problem of country – education – teacher unions – the rich opt out – it is a two-tier system.

Charlie: Omaha public school system - sign books in warehouse in South Omaha – 8th grade – books on tape – failure in a sense.

Warren: I have a friend who teaches kids to read – enthusiasm needed – started in Harlem.

Equality of opportunity – rich school vs public school.

Merger of Berkshire Hathaway and Microsoft? I keep hinting, but it does not work. (Big laugh from audience.)

Homebuilding – it is using somebody's savings even if zero down.

It became easier as prices went up.

Easy financing facilitated the boom.

Farm bubble was the same – they lent amounts above what the farm could sustain.

Bigger fool game.

Easy lending lowers savings.

Other countries are investing in U.S.

Charlie: Eventually they will construct too many houses – the price will go down.

Warren: Government guarantee on loans.

Charlie: Ponzi effects in the economy.

Warren: $35 - $400 gold compound rate is bad.

Business ability innate - how know? We buy businesses with good managers.

Can't look at MBA class and rank people on potential for success.

We take the easy way – we see they bat .350.

Best correlation of success - age at which the person started their first business.

We have some managers with MBAs - some not.

A lot can be improved, but some is wiring.

I've never heard Charlie say anything dumb about business.

Charlie: Part is intelligence and part is temperament.

Warren: Cologne Re – Gen Re owns 91%. We will buy the remaining 9% when it is offered to us.

Question: What about AIG?

Warren: No comment. Wait on 10K.

Charlie: AIG did a lot right. There was a lot of ability in that place. Hank Greenberg was tops in Insurance.

Warren: Freddie - housing – for fee of .25% - guarantee mortgage – it was looked at as a government guarantee – they got carried away – they tried to deliver rates of growth – they could not handle the risk of interest rate changes – carry trade accounting shenanigans – wanted earning-per- share to go up – contribute to Congress – consequences of company using government credit

Charlie: Used derivatives.

Warren: $5 billion mismarked in one direction – $9 billion mismarked in another direction

Question: Are you willing to buy in U.K.

Warren: Mid-American has big business in U.K.

U.K. has a rule – you have to report at 3%.

5 billion pounds - buy 150 million pounds, then report.

Had Guinness – they have a lot of rules in the U.K.

We like durable competitive advantage.

Management we like.

Good price.

Charlie: Odd occurrence – we have the currency of socialized countries in Europe.

Warren: There is slow growth in Europe.

U.S. 1.5% growth in population.

Obligation – intermediary in transaction – that party accounts.

Charlie: Ambiguities bar tender liability.

Radio station - sell advertising to people who have ads that lie.

Question: Individual select currency or stock for Dollar versus the Euro?

Warren: No.

Best - invest in your own ability.

Pay students $100,000 for 10% of their earnings.

Anything you do to develop your own abilities or own business is better.

Charlie: Don't do asset allocation.

Warren: We are out-of-step with modern investment management.

Charlie: If a thing is not worth doing at all, it is not worth doing well.

Warren: See--he is Ben Franklin!

Inflation and decline of dollar – have good business for in Florida.

Airlines are hurt by inflation.

Best protection - business does not require continual investment of capital.

We are always worried about inflation.

See's did ok with inflation.

Utility cost more.

Berkshire is ethical.

Bear market? Good opportunity to buy.

We will buy for as long as I live.

Charlie: Longer.

Warren: We spend no time thinking about what the market will do.

There is always a list of bad things.

I am an enormous bull on this country.

It does not make sense to bet against the U.S.

Charlie: Economy of U.S. increases for years. We are at or near the apex of a great civilization.

Warren: You heard it here first.

I have seen more people pass up a good opportunity because of bad news.

Question: What about GM and Ford – health care and insurance liability?

Answer: GM and Ford CEO's were handed different hands to play.

They have an inherent bad cost structure from contracts years ago.

Retirees cost is staggering.

Had 50% of auto market--now 25%.

$90 billion in pension fund.

$27 billion in health.

GM = $14 billion in equity.

No accounting consequences at the time.

Charlie: Gave optimistic prognosis.

Asbestos – Terrible behavior by Doctors, Lawyers, Courts, Politicians.

Warren: Diverse businesses. How successor manages/ creates climate where people who ran them continue to run them. GM and Coke bought some other businesses – did badly.

We have no group Vice Presidents, Headquarters Directives, HR Department, PR Department, or Law Department in Omaha.

Successor in Berkshire – they have seen it - believe in it. Easy to keep the engine going down the track at 90 mph. There are three possible successors.

Charlie: Lack of oversight is good.

Warren: We are a conglomerate.

Use simplicity.

Every share I have will go to the foundation.

Best investment - getting Charlie who works cheap.

See's was big in the past.

First half of GEICO for $40 million. Still growth potential.

I now have a GEICO credit card.

I pay it off (the card balance) each month.

Six million customers - GEICO.

Charlie: $2 billion second half GEICO.

Ajait Jain – best investment.

Warren: N.Y. Stock exchange shenanigans.

Think N.Y. Stock Exchange should be not-for-profit.

Enemy of investors gain is activity.

Activity is good for commissions.

Volume increase on exchange - frictional cost of capitalism.

Charlie: Lost our way. Stock Exchange had a duty to act as exemplar.

Warren: Social security introduced in '36 or '37.

My grandfather had Charlie bring two cents to work to pay for it.

It was proposed as insurance.

First woman put in $22 vs $2,400 she got out of it.

It is a transfer payment - not insurance.

Pay below present level – age – would be a mistake.

Rich country takes care of young and old.

Charlie and I are wired to get rich – it is not equal for an 85 IQ person.

401K dividend and capital gains - 15% - obligation to provide.

Quit tax at $90,000 – 12.4%

Don't want to hurt bottom 20%.

Question: Will there be a deficit in social security 25 years out?

Warren: $500 billion deficit now.

Four percent to social security now – six percent in 20 years.

Change – means test all income - increase retirement age.

Charlie: Right Wing Republican speaking – Republicans are out of their minds to take this on now. Hard to fake being dead. Leave it alone.

Warren: Freddie and Fannie difficult to analyze.

Insurance company loss adjustment account - we have $45 billion in loss reserves.

Question: Are bank loans any good?

Warren: Due diligence of agencies. Freddie and Fanny – 1 was $5 billion off/1 was $9 billion off.

Salomon board handled thousands of transactions – insurance, banking, finance companies; more dangerous field to analyze.

GEICO – more valid statistics.

Asbestos Insurance way off – wouldn't fault rating agencies.

Charlie: Warren is obviously correct – some of the worst

financial reporting is by the government.

Warren: In '68 and '69, I liquidated my partnership.

We do own some stock – would not buy at these prices.

We face huge costs going in and out – taxes, etc.

Like the businesses – lower percentage in stocks now.

Not unhappy with Coke, Amex, Wells Fargo, Moody's.

Charlie: Lately small numbers – millions.

Warren: Still doing ok.

But not nimble.

Can eventually do again at satisfactory rates.

Small is still billions.

Question: Would you consider buying gold?

Warren: Way down on my list.

I prefer 100-acres of land, or an apartment house, or an index fund.

Between1900 and 2000, gold went from $20 to $400.
In this same period, the Dow went from $60 to $13,000, plus dividends.

Problem with gold is that one has to pay for insurance and storage.

If you're worried about paper money, it is the last thing to own, if paper money is bad if trade in.

Seashells collect in that.

Charlie: Gold - good in Vienna in 1935 for a Jewish family.

Question: Can you discuss ten-year returns?

Warren: Every now and then we can say something on the market – '69, '74, and '99.

Now we are more into equities than the sum of '99.

Question: Which will do better in 20 years – long-term bonds or equities?

Warren: Equities.

More than 6 or 7%.

Question not in a bubble for equities or bargain area.

Will get a chance soon to do well in equities.

Real estate - Charlie started in real estate – tax disadvantage.

There is a bubble in real estate now.

Done well in real estate? None – REITS were cheap in '99.

Had 1% of net worth in REITS.

Now fancy prices on property and **REITS – overpriced now**.

Pay attention to something scorned, and then touted.

Charlie: They have phony accounting.

Warren: The more prosperous the rest of the world is, the better for us. Same with trade.

Charlie: Asia will do best in future.

Question: Will the dollar devalue?

Warren: Don't see how it can happen with stronger dollar, but could get chaotic markets--not Armageddon-type--absent terrorism, of course.

Citizens will be better off 10 years from now.

Buy a company so good an idiot could run it, because some day one will!

Real GDP per capita up seven times in one century in U.S.

Country will survive in spite of severe financial dislocations – we could have some opportunity.

Charlie: More chances for convulsion now.

Warren: Creation of new financial instruments, financial intermediaries – fund managers are all on a hair-trigger like fall of '98.

They could all head for the exit at one time.

Charlie: Amount of credit being used is way too heavy.

Puts and calls on individual stocks.

I had a friend with a $2.5 million house and $5 million in securities. He lost it all trading futures. He now works in a restaurant.

Warren: Anybody we have not offended?

Directors? Charlie, we are out of step.

Model concept for Directors is one from each diversity category and a $100,000 salary.

At Berkshire, we have the opposite. All our directors are rich and get no salary, but have a lot of stock in Berkshire.

Warren: In baseball, if you have a .240 hitter, you might get rid of him for a .280 hitter; whereas, with Directors - if they are mediocre, it is difficult to lead a change or lead a rump meeting to get rid of the CEO.

Independent – willingness, but not eagerness to challenge bad deals.

All ours (directors) have money in Berkshire they bought in the market.

All our directors are very smart.

We have the best Board in the country.

I never invest in Technology.

Question: Have you received pressure from Bill Gates to invest in Technology?

Warren: All kinds of pressure. Ha! Ha!

We will stay within our circle of competence.

I will listen to any idea he (Bill Gates) has.

Charlie: For the good – great Board.

The Director getting $150,000 a year from the company that needs it, is not independent.

Warren: I have never seen them be independent.

One Director was removed two times from the Compensation Committee because he questioned it.

Question: What criteria is best for financial returns?

Warren: Financial returns are a gauge, but don't get rid of a company if it doesn't meet it--unless it is a continual loser - or it has labor problems.

Business School theory or Management theory says get rid of it; not every investment will run perfectly – some unexpected conditions.

Charlie: We will reject some on moral grounds.

Warren: We would own the stock of a cigarette company, but we would not own the whole company.

Looked at a Memphis company – good company, but we did not want to be in that business.

Charlie: We were young and poor. **It was like putting $100 million in a bushel basket and setting it on fire.**

I did not want to do it.

Warren: Read the book, _Poor Charlie's Almanac._

Question: How about Pharmaceutical companies?

Warren: We don't know much in the political realm.

Charlie: I Share Warren's agnosticism on it. **Throw it into the "too hard" pile and move on.**

Warren: There is no degree of difficulty in the Investment world.

We get paid for not jumping over a seven foot bar, but stepping over a one-foot bar.

Question: How about emotional traps?

Warren: Recognize traps. Our personnel are not so prone to these mistakes; they make fewer mistakes than others.

You don't have to out run the bear – just out run the other fellow.

10-year rate 4.2% - staying short on bonds.

Question: Is Reinsurance finite?

Warren: All Insurance is finite – has a limit.

Non-traditional Insurance sector - looking at retroactive contract in - sold to ACE – pay $2.5 billion in claims, get premium $1.5 billion – had value to both parties.

Authorities - looking for contracts that had no purpose or had bad accounting.

Insurance is all about risk.

Charlie: Reinsurance for Financial Reports.

Warren: $400 billion in Insurance premiums paid each year.

Question: Most difficult decision?

Charlie: Shouldn't ask or you give examples.

Warren: Difficult – can't think of – bad – yes – like umpire calls balls and strikes – have to make instant decision – if don't - get fired.

Question: Please discuss Real Estate Brokerage Power House?

Warren: Build on model of today. Residential – $50 billion; last year, second largest broker in the U.S.

One-on-one important vs Internet.

Millions of homes sold each year.

Big and local will be bigger in five to 10 years.

Logical buyer – good owner – discount reserve – pay in future – discount back to now - could make that argument but management so understated reserves - leave as is.

Question: What about Longtail business – derivatives?

Warren: Mind boggling to implement.

Trader estimate higher than actual – we inherited 23,000 derivative contracts.

We are unwinding them now – over three years.

No auditor or regulator can understand them.

Charlie: Stupid and dishonorable accountants let genie out of the bottle.

Warren: Derivatives – people think everything is ok.

It is like a guy who jumps off the 40th floor and he thinks everything is ok, as he goes by the 20th floor.

Chapter 6

On May 6, 2006, 24,000 shareholders attended the annual Berkshire meeting at the Qwest Center in Omaha, Nebraska.

In the Exhibit Hall, we saw Warren sitting on the fancy GEICO motorcycle. And, of course, playing his ukulele.

The movie was funny with Warren giving Tiger Woods golf pointers.

Warren: "Anna Nicole Smith Rule" – When choosing between two old rich guys, pick the older one! (This, after a skit in the movie where Desperate Housewives are trying to get Warren as their boyfriend, but end up with Charlie.)

Lliberty's Kids - American History.

Secret millionaires club.

See's Candy - purchased in 1972.

Park Century School.

Jamie Lee Curtis.

GEICO – good growth first quarter.

Acquisition – ISCAR – Israel.

They are the best in their field.

They are young.

They have 5,000 employees.

They manufacture metal-processing cutting tools.

We paid $4 billion for 80% of the company.

Their family owns the remaining 20%.

Business Meeting will be from 3:15 to 3:16 p.m.

At 4 p.m., there will be the International Meeting.

Question: Social security – how take care of old and young?

Warren: Question with every country – age 65 may be outmoded – $40,000 GDP per person.

We are wired to do well.

Our Country can easily handle it. Maintain present age. Problem growing pie.

Charlie: Grow 3% per annum; easy to get more money. Could pay more in the future.

Warren: This is what happens when you ask old guys.

90

Boom/bust cycle – Copper now $3.50 was $.80.

Measure by cost of production.

Tie to what is under control of Manager.

GEICO growth and seasonal business.

Oil company - find cheaply.

Charlie: Half of companies have unfair compensation system – too high.

Warren: Berkshire has 68 operating companies, 40 managers, and 40 years of no-compensation-consultant.

I was on one compensation committee.

Charlie: At Solomon, Warren softly suggested the idea of compensation; he was outvoted. It is not because of greed, but envy.

Warren: Envy you feel worse.

Question: Are you actively training successors?

Warren: Our culture is the training. No formal lessons.

We have three obvious candidates to take my place.

Charlie: Do you think Warren is going to blow the job of succession?

Warren: We don't train managers. We find them.

You can look at Everest and know it is a high mountain.

Question: What about Emerging Markets?

Warren: Closed end funds with premium – irrational – most closed end funds go to discounts – pay 6% premium – why? I have seen 30 or 40.

Charlie: I have nothing to add.

Warren: He is hitting his stride now.

Frank RVs.

Plurality vs majority voting for board members.

Charlie: No different.

Warren: What percentage think like owners – dual voting doesn't change it.

The job of the Board is to get the right CEO, see that he does not over reach, and watch acquisitions. This is the only cure--large shareholders zero in on these issues. Big, large institutional investors farmed out their voting.

Learning about Tech – **know what you don't know.**

Know your circle of competence.

Telecom – huge change.

3 boxes, in (yes), out (no), too hard Charlie says.

Tom Watson (IBM) said – I'm no genius, but I'm smart in spots and I stay around those spots.

I was there at the birth of Intel. On the board of Grinnell

College. Bought $300,000 of bonds.

Charlie: A foreign correspondent once said, "You guys don't look smart enough to do this much better. How do you do it?" I said that **we know the edge of our circle of competence.**

Warren: Median family income – corporate income – all capital assets in U.S.

Corporate profits are high, but corporate income tax is not that high.

Median family income.

We are not shooting for tax breaks for the wealthy.

High 2005 return - no tax shelters - 2004 lowest tax rate in the office.

Charlie: GDP per capita going up – huge flux up and down.

Question: What about ethanol?

Warren: Ethanol? We have been approached on it.

We don't know.

It is easy to raise money for it now.

It is hot.

Ag Processing has not been a great business.

Charlie: Thermodynamics. It takes more fossil fuel to get it.

Question: Is there a commodity bubble?

Warren: Problem in copper now – speculation.

What the wise man does in the beginning, the fool does in the end.

Tulip Bulbs - famous – envy your neighbor.

Charlie: Our history shows how good we are.

Question: What about Silver?

Warren: We sold off our Silver early. At the end, it turns into pumpkins and mice (you are at the Ball having drinks and dancing, and the girls are getting prettier, but at the end, it all turns into pumpkins and mice).

Question: What about the International market?

Warren: South American stock market.

Berkshire has a $135 billion market value. We have to put a lot to work to move the needle.

Petro China – $400 million in - now worth $2 billion.

One needs a great manager.

Manufactured housing industry – volume low - last couple of years – some years 20% - last year 7% of new housing stock – our houses are better quality - $45 per square foot – some areas we develop subdivisions – a few years ago abuse of credit – sold to people not credit worthy – Clayton's position – strong.

Charlie, MiTek helps with stick-built.

Warren: Clayton could be the largest home builder in the U.S.

someday.

Bad credit in stick-built now.

Bad lending – Dumb lending - plus terrible accounting.

Russia stock – While at Solomon, we got in on oil in Siberia. We dug holes – we did not get the oil.

Residential – California – 20 years $5 – 6; $100 million now – cashed out too soon. Slowing down now. Day-trading real estate. Florida - $500,000 condos now – glut now – higher end down – differs by region.

We have $37 billion in cash.

We want $10 billion as a rule.

We spent $4 billion on Iscar.

We are working on a $15 billion deal, but it may not come to fruition.

It is likely to take us three years to get down to $10 billion in cash.

But we don't want a stupid deal.

Coke volume goes up every year.

Insurance rates up.

Can lose billions in any event – but ok.

Can pay on a $150 billion event – Our share would be $4 billion.

On balance sheet – Two billion different charges on retroactive policies, reinsurance losses – amortize over time.

Net Jets expense over revenue – biggest in the world, but bet it will be making money soon.

Silver – we had a lot – but we don't now.

Silver – byproduct of copper production.

We have none now.

It does not produce for you.

In the TV ad, the GEIGO gecko has an Australian accent.

Region with high resources per capita – too macro for us.

Terrorist – nuclear bomb in U.S. city? It will happen.

Somebody might sell metal derivatives.

We (U.S.) probably have intercepted some bombs.

Good read is *Poor Charlie's Almanac.*

Question: Will you buy back Berkshire stock?

Warren: Most of the time one can't buy enough to have anything meaningful happen.

Berkshire has the lowest turnover of shareholders. They think of themselves as owners.

Helpers – bad.

Charlie: Reduce expectations.

Warren: In aggregate, investment professional does not add value; however $140 billion is spent on it every year.

A great business is a University Business School - charge $50,000 per student per semester.

Question: What about illegal immigrants?

Warren: Problem should be addressed for citizenship.

Need to enforce rules.

Charlie: Get used to it.

Warren: Forty schools visit us at a time.

Teaching has improved some from a low base 25 years ago.

You couldn't get a job if you didn't say efficient market theory or general portfolio theory.

Difficult if everybody in the world runs a hedge fund.

Charlie: Half of the grads in eastern schools want to go into hedge funds – do you want to measure your success vs a junior counterpart in Goldman Sachs?

Warren: My successor will have media probation – one year or two years; then see.

Culture the same.

CEO – Half and half doesn't work well for us.

Charlie: Munger heirs want to wring greatest amount out of Warren.

Warren: New CEO will know how to make good deals and avoid bad deals.

Question: How do you pick a church or school for Capital allocation to charity?

Warren: I look for an important cause that isn't funded.

Pick what makes you happy.

We get the profit of one out of every 12 Cokes.

Utilities - return of capital.

In Energy field, we follow the will of the people in various states.

Media vs Internet. 2 eyeballs – 24 hours per day – 50 years ago 3 ways to get information – now way more.

More ways – more competition – eroding profits.

Charlie: I have a friend in the newspaper business and her idea of competition is a corpse laid out on a slab with one toe twitching.

Warren: Hard to see them (newspapers) getting better.

World Book - $300,000 at $600 each in '80's.

Currency – view not so much in money futures – other ways - like Iscar – large earnings not in dollars – U.S. dollar will continue to weaken.

Charlie: Currency trading was a non-event.

Warren: Well, I made a couple billion dollars with it. If it's not a big thing to him (Charlie), he can give his share to me! (Big laugh from the audience.)

Balance of trade – soft landing – I don't get it.

Big adjustment someday.

CPI – measure of inflation – not very good.

Russell Business Wire.

Med Pro.

Pacific Corps.

We get books with silly projections. I would like to bet the guy who made the book on the projection coming true.

Applied Underwriters.

Keep 19%.

Iscar – $4 billion deal – no investment banker.

Charlie: Deal flippers are getting in each others way.

Role models for integrity and common sense.

Warren: Derivative meltdown – how – don't know.

Long Term Capital Management.

Newspapers – multiples too high – declining business – take people to cemetery – taking a newspaper reader.

A new graduate from high school is not a new newspaper

reader.

A newspaper is a pre-prints wrapper.

Question: Who were your mentors?

Warren: Tom Murphy, Don Keough.

Charlie: We are not following 40-year old's careers.

Warren: Investment is not tough – you need the courage of your convictions.

Most people were paralyzed in the early '70s.

We bought a lot.

In 2002, all were terrified to act.

Question: If you had $1 million, how invest?

Warren: May 4, 1956, started first partnership.

You only need one good idea.

Charlie started in development.

I do stocks.

I look for something very mispriced that I understand.

Charlie: Look for the best you can find.

Modern portfolio theory is asinine! Find 1,000 equally good things – not possible.

Book author? He is demented. He is comparing apples to

100

elephants.

Warren: Ben Graham said, "You are neither right nor wrong because somebody agrees or disagrees with you."

Knowable and important – market is there to serve you – not instruct you.

You can't miss.

Charlie: Some of you can miss. (Big laugh from audience.)

Warren: Annual Report – we put in what we would want to know.

If you are a serious owner, read the whole report.

Look at businesses we have and the type we might add.

Question: What will Berkshire be worth in 10 years from now?

Warren: Look at earnings.

Charlie: With many complex tasks - do the easy ones first – no brainers.

Warren: Insurance – redeploy excess insurance cash.

Develop float – $48 or $49 billion.

Hard to do more. Can't grow at a large rate.

In bankruptcy, we first bought the bonds of Fruit of the Loom from bankruptcy.

Charlie: Courts are in competition with each other to get bankruptcy cases. If they overpay, they get more business.

Warren: We look at it.

We tripled money – bought Enron bonds after bankruptcy.

Big complicated mess.

Some things to do.

P&G growth – consumer powerhouse.

Gillette – stronger than anybody.

Big retailers own brands is a problem.

Good together.

P&G drug business – don't know.

Oriental Trading Company for sale – Berkshire interest?

Private group buys and wants to resell – strategic buyer equals buyer to pay too much.

Fund A sells to Fund B, to Fund C, to Fund D – 20% take each time.

Earn more on assets outside U.S. than outside earn on assets in U.S.

Charlie: People like U.S. in spite of its faults.

Question: What's the difference between gambling and insurance business?

Warren: Gambling is a created risk. Home is existing risk.

Is there anyone we forgot to insult?

Illegal naked short selling (don't have the stock to produce)?
We don't care if they short Berkshire. They will have to buy it;
tough way to make a living. Tough on the gut.

We would never put money with a short fund.

Chapter 7

On May 5, 2007, 27,000 shareholders attended the Berkshire meeting at the Qwest Center in Omaha, Nebraska. Despite rain and lightning, it seems everyone had come early to line up and wait to get inside.

In the Exhibit Hall, we met the woman from Johns Manville who rode next to us on the flight from Denver to Omaha (small world). The CEO introduced himself to us and we looked at the Menard race car that Manville sponsors. We also got pictures with the Manville team.

We looked at the not-so-docile-looking long-horned steer at the Justin Boots display. We also saw Warren play his ukulele on the Justin Boots stage.

The movie started out with a cartoon of long-haired hippies (Warren and Charlie) driving their "love-in van" to Woodstock – err Berkstock. They were selling tie-dyed shirts, but no one was buying. Finally, Janis Joplin stopped by and traded some poem lyrics for one. Charlie and Warren then traded all the shirts for Coke; then traded for See's candy.

The next segment featured the "Gipper" (Ronald Regan); and Nebraska football highlights with Johnny Rodgers, Tommy Frazier, and Matt Davison. Warren's office staff was dressed up in football gear – shoulder pads and helmets - and as they started work, they jumped up to touch a sign that said "Play Like a Champion Today."

Warren played basketball one-on-one with Le Bron James of the Cleveland Cavs. Warren *somehow* won.

The movie ended with the Coke song playing, while Susie sang the changed lyrics and the pictures of all the Berkshire CEOs flashed across the screen.

We later met Marla Gottschalk, CEO of Pampered Chef, in the Exhibit Hall. A nicer woman you could not meet. We talked about the Pampered Chef line, since my wife was about to attend a Pampered Chef party back home. Believe me; we will never bypass this booth ever again, as we learned they always feature a wonderful product, at a reduced cost, which sells out very quickly prior to the meeting.

Warren and his daughter Susie sat in the audience watching the movie in their usual seats half way down the basketball floor from the stage and movie screen.

Several minutes after the movie ended, they dimmed the lights and announced the great Mr. Buffett coming out on the stage. Out came Jimmy Buffet in a Hawaiian shirt, shorts, and sandals, and with his guitar. He said he'd had a DNA test and he would therefore be Warren's successor. He played "Margaritaville," but the words were changed to be about Berkshire Hathaway.

Warren: Cartoon for kids – financial education.

My daughter Susie put together the movie.

Charlie is hyperkinetic – he is on his medicine.

Kim Chase – his father helped me take control of Berkshire.

Insurance business was extraordinary – nothing bad happened.

Lag effect – insurance results will go down.

Hope to break even over time on underwriting. Generate float. Float is at an all-time high.

Residential construction - lower earnings.

Bubble in finding deals.

Private equity doesn't burst.

If private equity buys a business – $20 billion – do a poor job – it still takes many years to see it - not like stocks.

If yields on junk bonds go up, then slow down deals.

Private Equity Fund – 2% fee = $400 million on $20 billion – ($400 million is real money in Omaha) they invest it quickly - get another fund going so get more fees.

Charlie: It can continue to go on for a long time, even after a state of revulsion sets in.

Warren: The voice of pessimism sets in.

Question: What about International investing?

Warren: Did 50 years ago.

Own stock in two in Germany and 4% in Korea.

Have to report what we hold at $300 million in Germany and U.K.

Executive compensation is bad, but the wrong manager is worse by far.

To the Compensation Committee, it is play money.

They (CEOs) are looking for cocker spaniels with their tails wagging--not Dobermans.

Envy is the worst of the seven deadly sins because you feel bad.

I have two Net Jets shares.

Charlie has one. I shamed him into it.

Using Net Jets is a real asset to Berkshire.

Manager compensation – pay for things that they can control and we care about.

Pay for lowest finding cost.

Charlie: If you get too enchanted with the trappings of power, it is bad.

Warren: Fudge diet is good.

Credit contraction in times of chaos is good for us.

Problem is there is no contraction in credit.

If it happens in the market, it is good for us.

Federal Reserve was established to smooth it out.

Charlie: Last time there was a credit contraction, we made $3 or $4 billion.

Warren: '98 fall - seize up - panic - Long Term Capital Management went down.

Charlie: John Adams and his wife were wonderful people.

Warren: Did you know them personally?

Corporate profit was 4-6% of GDP – now 8% of GDP – could be higher taxes – may go up.

Earn 20% - bonds 4% - corporate tax rates were 52% - now 35% - some 20%

Banks earn 1.5% on assets = 20% - can't continue

Here at Berkshire, we have a diverse group of great managers – something probably going on – but have culture that minimizes problems.

Managers – no quarterly reports required – would give managers opportunity to hide losses to make "Warren" look good on Wall Street – pressure to make numbers, etc.

Cheap stock prices – result – think about what bad can happen.

Question: What if Wall Street fails to deliver stock or naked shorts?

Warren: I have no problem with shorts.

We make money.

We lent our stock of USG to short sellers.

Sue broker if no certificate, Charlie?

Charlie: No.

Warren: I'll get somebody else to represent me.

Gambling stocks – have good futures.

Day trading is gambling.

I watch the weather channel. It is exciting.

If you make it easy, more people will gamble.

Gambling is a tax on ignorance.

State lottery – government preys on the weakness of its citizenry.

Charlie: Casinos use clever psychological tricks to get people.

Berkshire won't have a casino.

Warren: Read everything you can.

By age 10, I had read every book in the Omaha Public Library on investing.

You must jump into the water.

It is like reading a romance novel vs doing something else.

At 19, I read the book, *The Intelligent Investor.*

Reading will set the framework.

You will see what jumps out at you.

To a job applicant – Sandy Gottesman would ask – what do you own? Why do you own it?

You own a business – take a yellow pad – 100 shares of GM at 30 – why buy GM for $180 billion?

Why? Do you have a margin of safety?

We favor businesses where we know the answer.

Great businesses don't need a large margin of safety.

We may pay close to $1 on $1 for a great business.

If a person walks in the door at 300 or 320 pounds, you know they are fat!

A fat business you know!

Buy a good business at a reasonable price.

Charlie: It is high school algebra.

If you don't know it, take up another profession.

Warren: Health care – too tough. We can't fix it.

We look for easy stuff.

Look for low distribution cost.

Low frictional cost.

Intrinsic value is based on the future cash of the business discounted back to the present.

Try to give present value – marketable securities – retained earnings – how use?

In 1965, the textile business was $12 per share – but not the whole story.

Used retained earnings to buy other businesses.

Put to work now and in the future has greater worth.

$80,000 in marketable securities per share.

Charlie: Hard to judge past vs future balance sheet gross.

Why? This young man (Warren) is a learning machine.

He has improved.

Warren: There is a big advantage to practice in this field.

Pass CEO mantle from 65 year old to 59 year old – bad.

People in place now to continue.

Derivatives – bad accounting.

Accountants said you don't understand accounting.

Four big audit firms in this country.

I wish we had sold our derivatives to the accountants.

Wildly different valuations on both sides.

Charlie: There will be a big denouement.

Sigma people are stupid.

They believe in the tooth fairy.

Easy to teach using advanced math that none but the priesthood can do.

No utility.

Counter utility.

Warren, Aesop – 600 BC – A bird in the hand is worth two in the bush.

Fundamentals of investing:

Know when know.

Know when don't.

Most ideas go in the too-hard pile.

We can recognize one-foot bars.

We can step over one-foot bars.

Not looking for someone to teach.

We have 600 applications for my job.

We want good investment records.

Will they (applicants) scale up?

Can they run $100 billion vs $100 million?

I will not blow it.

Charlie: Mozart – a 25 year old asks him how he writes symphonies. Mozart says you are too young. The 25-year old reminds him that he did it at age 10. Mozart says, "Yes, but I was not asking for advice on how to do it."

Warren: In 1969, I found three people to manage my partners' money.

We can do it again.

In 1979, I met Lou Simpson. It was clear in one hour – he was the man.

Global warming may be a problem.

Our business – Gen-Re – no effect.

General Indemnity – more.

Raise premiums – make more money.

Charlie: plants eat CO2 – warm is better than cold – it is not utter catastrophe.

You have to be a pot-smoking journalism student to believe in it (man-made global warming).

Warren: We don't know all the factors in hurricanes.

Chinese banking system is like Japan in the '90's.

We don't know.

We were offered Chinese banks.

We said no.

Charlie: Fifteen years adverse Chinese banking practices – make you shudder. They have been doing it for years.

Warren: Frank Martin – good book.

If you ran an endowment fund? Prospective return on municipal bonds were equal – now not same – it would be all stock or all bonds.

Buy index 500 for 20 years – buy without fees.

Disruption nice if have cash.

We bought $5 billion of equities in the first quarter.

We don't predict the future.

Silver markets – we bought too early – sold too early –other than that, we did perfect.

No silver conspiracy – supply and demand.

I thought my wife would give away the money.

(In donating the money) I haven't given up anything.

I want to keep doing what I enjoy doing.

If I had a small sum, I would do things differently.

There would be one thousand times more options to look at.

High returns on small sums.

Managed future funds? Berkshire better.

Just one segment is limited. Shrink universe of possibilities.

No formula produces results – manager does.

Charlie: Results between lousy and negative.

Warren: I agree. It is a sales tool to get the public will to buy.

Question: Young man – how do well?

Warren: Read everything on investing.

Talk to smart people – like I did with Lorimar Davidson of GEICO.

Ability to recognize – Long Term Capital Management – some fail – ways to make money – think 8-10 hours a day how.

Get a program.

Don't do anything where you can lose a lot.

Charlie: Look in inefficient markets.

Warren: REITS – won't guess up or down.

RTC seller - billion dollars worth of real estate – no lending – no economic interest – government was selling – they were eager to wind-up the job.

Won't be a scarcity of opportunities.

Insurance Florida? If people are mad and the government steps in – wind and water – socialize it – bad.

Nebraska pay for it – bad.

Bought $5.3 billion in the first quarter – did you change your standards? No – still have money to buy an elephant.

If you have no date for a month, then go out with a girl, did you change your standards?

Volatility vs risk? Volatility is not a measure of risk.

Volatility was Nebraska farm land – was it riskier at $600/ac than $2,000/ac?

Stupid teachers take math they learned and use it on nonsense.

Comes from not knowing what you are doing.

1% or ½% loss in stocks max.

Beta = volatility – not useful.

Charlie: Most investment management courses are 50% twaddle.

Early we recognized very smart people do very dumb things.

We avoid them.

Warren: I look for quality and integrity of management.

I bought many things where I never talked to management.

Read annual reports.

Read about the business.

Read about its competitors.

Large oil company – If you read their annual report, you can't find the "finding" cost of oil in the report.

Dishonest phrases in report only.

We have bought into good businesses run by people we did not like.

A good business will carry a bad manager.

Charlie: Don't look for Warrens under every bush.

Warren: A good manager can't fix a bad business.

Berkshire – lean and fat 17-year periods of equities.

Beyond 4-¾%, you don't need an opinion every day.

In '74 all cheap – buy.

Klamath River dams – salmon fishing – Pacific Corps – Mid-American Energy – FERC has 27 proposals – some like hydro power – clean cheap – it will be determined by FERC.

We are a public utility – we do public policy.

First dam 1906.

Merge New York Stock Exchange with Euromart - would be positive – it would narrow the spread – cost of execution – commissions lower.

Question: How do you know you are trusting the right people?

Warren: I get letters all the time from people who have been taken advantage of – frictional costs.

People give themselves away – clues what they talk about – I am deeply suspicious when what they say is too good to be true.

Like - We only insure concrete bridges under water.

What they laugh at.

They say it is easy.

Discount rates – don't have a formula – spread sheet.

Government bond rate – 2% don't do – 3.5% hurdle rate – don't say it.

Think about why one investment option is better than another.

Opportunity cost – presenters' present nonsense figures.

If he promises 20%, run him off.

Too difficult pile - ok for investments.

Other problems in life you can't ignore--like terminal illness.

Frequency of review – now more money than ideas – then all the time.

Continuous process – keep adding to knowledge.

Use information collected daily - then think of selling less desirable to buy most desirable – buy more.

We look at it all the time.

May go up by billions a year.

Will sell least attractive.

Buy 30-40% of daily trade.

Coke reporting problems – we can buy 20% of the daily trading volume and not change the price.

We are a big ocean liner.

We put in a lot of wind power in Iowa.

Klamath River – the world wants its electricity – 27 groups want different things.

FERC will decide.

Katrina – State of Florida - legislature insures its citizens.

Risk goes from private to public market.

Role models – they have not let me down.

Choosing heroes very important.

Charlie: Some of the best people are dead.

Ethanol – even McCain has had a counter revelation – thinks it is great because Iowa does. I think it is dumb. It raises the cost of food. **It is stupid Why would you put your food in**

your car to run it?

Warren: I love Nebraska.

Read *Supermoney.*

Question: What would be protection against Inflation?

Warren: Best protection is your own earning power.

Own a wonderful business – Coke, Snickers, Hershey.

Try to own good businesses.

Railroad industry – competitive position has improved.

As oil price goes up; it is more cost for truckers.

Railroad was a terrible business 30 years ago; better now.

It is a capital-intensive business.

Question: How can a ten-year old make money?

Warren: Deliver newspapers.

I tried 20 different businesses by the time I got out of high school.

Pin Ball business was the best.

Business success vs different variables – best correlation with the age you start your first business – the younger the better.

I often thought people in debt should do a paper route for extra money.

Charlie: I read *The Richest Man in Babylon*; it said **under-spend your income, then invest the difference.**

Warren: My advice to young people--become a reliable person. If you do, you won't fail in what you are trying to do.

My mother was from West Point, Nebraska.

If it has a big labor cost and can be built overseas, we don't want it.

Airlines bad. USAir. Shoe business.

Charlie: Will Rogers said we should be able to learn to not pee on an electrified fence without trying it.

Warren: We did $21 billion in foreign currency. Then the carry-rate got too high.

Now we buy some companies overseas.

Policies in this country will keep the decline of the dollar going.

Costco has had inflation of costs in store of zero.

Oil - $30 per barrel to $60 per barrel.

Euro .83 to 1.35.

Other countries are smarter about currencies.

Board of Directors' interaction. Many Boards of Directors were potted plants.

CEO did not want input.

CEO wants to be boss.

He doesn't want input from Board.

Job of Board is to have the right CEO.

No over-reaching by CEO.

Independent judgment of big acquisitions.

Consultant - investment banker present good deal.

Charlie: Most big deals are contrary to shareholder's interest.

Warren: I never hear "weigh what you give" versus "what you get."

Gave 20% of Berkshire to buy Dexter shoes. Dumb deal.

Gillette – 10 deals – bad.

Charlie: Self-serving delusional state.

Warren: Data documents – good Board - think like owners.

We have a sensational Board.

They have a large percent of their net worth in Berkshire.

Partners for deals? Don't want any.

Don't need the money or brains.

Want 100% for us.

Question: How about commodities?

Warren: No opinion.

Question: What about oil stock?

Warren: Good, but no opinion on oil going up.

Pasco – great steel company – bought at 3-5 times earnings.

We want a business that does not require a lot of capital.

See's Candy is better than an oil or steel company.

N.Y. Times – Schulzbergers – long suffering stock holders of N.Y. Times – woes of the business not because of the different classes of stocks.

Inertia from the past.

Circulation of the L.A. Times is going down.

World Book circulation was 300,000; now 22,000.

Buffalo News earnings are down 40%.

Dual structure of N.Y. Times was set up when it went public.

Chapter 8

On May 3, 2008, 31,000 stockholders converged on the Qwest Center in Omaha, Nebraska (quite a jump from the 10,000 at our first convention).

Before the doors opened, a painter entertained the crowd outside the arena by splashing paint on a moving canvas to music, while painting a modern art picture of Warren (to be auctioned off in the Exhibit Hall for charity).

When the doors finally opened, we rushed to get seats and then went to the Exhibit Hall. We had our picture taken with the GEICO racing team in front of their huge speed racing boat.

Before the movie, Warren took his usual seat halfway back on the main floor with a mystery woman in white who later turned out to be Susan Lucci of All My Children Soap Opera.

The movie had Walter Cronkite as the newscaster, with Charlie Munger running for president against Hillary Clinton.

Next, came a British parody of our current sub-prime mortgage debacle. The British tongue-in-cheek parody was too funny for words. The alleged high brow discussion had one Briton explaining the chain of events in America (the expert) to the interviewer. The "expert" explained that our U.S financial experts found bums on the street in stream vests (fishing vests), and gave them mortgages on houses they had no visible means of paying for. They then packaged together hundreds of similar mortgages, and sold them to investors. Then the "homeowners" default and the thousands of investors holding the mortgages are left holding the bag. The government then intercedes to "help" out, as so many people lose their houses which the banks can't sell.

Next, Warren calls Charlie and tells him he wants to buy Internet stocks--which Charlie nixes. So, Warren calls Jamie Lee Curtis (who both he and Charlie have a "thing for") to intercede. Jamie Lee is in bed seemingly naked. Warren begs her to call Charlie and make him agree. When she calls, Charlie is on the phone with his wife, but immediately hangs up. Charlie talks to Jamie Lee, who has to say very little to get him to agree to buy the Internet stocks.

After the movie, Susan Lucci of the All My Children Soap Opera comes out on the stage and sits in Warren's spot on the dais. She tells Charlie that she is the new Berkshire CEO. Come to find out, Warren also has a "thing" for her. She announces a new policy to consider issuing dividends, and Charlie asks if Warren approved. And she says that, as the new CEO, it's her decision. Warren then steps out from behind the curtain and rescinds her contract. This gets a very big laugh.

Charlie: He wants you to tell him to be less like a lemming.

Warren: What changed me? I started investing at age 11.

I started reading about it at age 6.

Read *The Intelligent Investor* at age 19, while at the University of Nebraska.

You can't get bad results if you follow it.

Cousin Bill Buffett has a book out about the grocery store.

Three lessons part of business.

Use the market to serve you.

Margin of safety.

Cologne Re 95% owned subsidiary of Gen-Re.

We will own 100% soon.

They ran their own investment portfolio.

I will take it over.

Recession – stock market – don't know.

I look at all companies – ignore 99.5% of them.

I buy stock – would be happy if they closed the market.

If you buy a farm outside of Omaha, look at what it would produce.

Charlie: Nothing to add.

Warren: He has been practicing for weeks.

Question: How do you find a good manager?

Warren: Thirty-five classes of MBAs come to Omaha.
We cheat and buy good businesses with great managers in place.

Our Mangers are independently wealthy.

We gave them a check for a billion or hundred million dollars.

Do they love the business--or love the money?

We see passion in their eyes.

Look for a passion.

Mrs. B. worked until age 103. When she left, she died the next year – that is a lesson to our other managers – don't quit on us.

Question: Do you recommend Stock or options?

Warren: One time we sold "puts" on Coke. Just buy the stock; that is better than a call option. Don't use it to get stock.

Charlie: Turn market into gambling parlor, so make croupier more money. Wrong.

Warren: They should tell MBAs how to value a business.

Question: How do you think about stock market fluctuations?

Warren: Not formulas.

College teachers want to teach what they know *and what you don't.*

Instead, buy a good business at a good price.

Question: Do you find joys in giving?

Warren: I have not given much away.

Giving away excess is not like a person with little money giving.

Sister Doris here gives a lot, plus time.

Ethical problem? Let Manager run the business.

Question: Is Fruit of the Loom a sweat shop in South America?

Warren: It is not a sweat shop.

Letter every two years who their successor would be.

No budgets – no quarter numbers to hit.

In the U.S., 1 billion pairs of shoes a year used to be manufactured. Now, all outside of U. S.

Tungsten price go up in China.

Built plant in China to serve China, not because of price change.

Higher value-added product.

No substitutes.

Raw materials – pass through most cost. Carpet business –slow because of the housing market, but little squeezes not a big deal.

Iscar exceeds all my expectations.

Don't like inflation, but will make more money over time with inflation.

Buy stock – get 7-10% return? Yes.

Market cap $10 billion or $50 billion and up.

$10 billion buy $500 million – double pay tax - .2 of 1% of BRK profit – nice but doesn't move the needle.

If you have a small amount of money and time to study, you can find better stocks.

Now, we buy big businesses – they give us capital.

Dam and fish – up to FERC.

Question: How is your health?

Warren: Good mental health with our job.

I have a trainer three times a week for 45 minutes.

Charlie is 84 – I am 77.

Don't look at minuses.

Charlie: We have no dietary rules.

I don't plan to change.

Warren: We associate with wonderful people.

A 10-million-dollar retention bonus for a CEO is ridiculous.

Question: If you were to start over, what would you do?

Warren: I would pick this job.

You find what is your passion.

I found mine early.

My dad was in the business, and books I read turned me on before Playboy.

If my dad was a minister, I would not have been as excited.

I worked for Ben Graham for two years and loved it.

It is important who you marry.

Charlie: Passion for something you have an aptitude for.

Question: Do you have advice for quiet people?

Warren: I faced it in high school. I was terrified of public speaking – avoided classes that required it – got physically ill. Then, I took the Dale Carnegie class and volunteered to teach at the University of Nebraska at Omaha, just for the public-speaking experience.

I signed up for the class in Washington D.C. – paid $100 by check – then went home and stopped payment on the check. I later gave $100 in cash in Omaha for the class, so I couldn't back out.

I was quite introverted.

Force yourself into it.

Get into a similar group.

Simple and important – not foolish and unimportant.

Another question about Klamath Dam.

Warren: Public Utilities Commission will decide.

Iowa – wind farms – some don't like wind – use of land – we get fair return on coal, wind, water.

There is blue-green algae in many lakes in the U.S. and Canada.

1964 letter = pair trading? Yes - did - long one short the other – Ben Graham in 1920s hedge fund concept – four out of five times, it worked.

Borrow stocks from university – NYU - long on attractive stock – short market – not a big deal – better just buy the stock.

Charlie: Long in the good business--not scheme.

Warren: Subprime market – dislocations – many ways to take advantage of.

Tax exempt money – market funds – every seven days, reprice bonds in them.

1/24 3.1 4.0 3.5.

2/14 8.0 10.0 4.2.

Huge dislocation.

We have to bid at 11.3%.

Found in 98 and 94.

$4 billion in this now.

We will make some money on it.

Charlie: Brief time available – municipal bonds were – think fast – act resolutely.

Warren, 2002 junk bond market – small business get big.

Berkshire was small at one time.

No Master Plan to get big.

We will get bigger.

Not gallop to big.

Most small businesses will not get big.

All big businesses will become mediocre.

Ajit Jain was our best investment.

$400 million from municipal bond insurances 1st quarter – larger than all other companies combined.

Financial Statement - Look at only what look at – understand the business? No, most of the time.

Know the financial past – know the future – not offer unless know the business.

Most times don't talk to management.

Charlie: We like to drown in cash businesses.

Warren: Like businesses that mail you a check.

When we buy a business, it is less of a bargain than when we buy a stock.

If I landed from Mars with 1 billion in Mars money, I would not put it in U.S. money.

Don't hedge currencies.

Small sums – investor has thousands of possibilities.

Mispriced bonds, stocks, U.S. and foreign.

Ridiculously cheap.

Not currencies, tax liens.

Tom Knapp did.

I would pay to have this job.

The boom in the price of farm products (crops) made the food prices go up.

Candidates say what they do because of the political process.

At Berkshire, we have three CEO candidates who are all better than me.

As far as Investment officers, four are all better than me.

All are young and rich--tomorrow or five years from now.

Charlie: Young man here - Warren Buffett - encourage him to reach his full potential.

We are aging at a slow rate.

Put a lot of money in one idea?

Warren: We have had 75% or more in one idea.

You will see some things it would be a mistake to not have 50% in – 2500% - bad.

Berkshire was not a cinch.

2002 junk bonds.

1974 Cap Cities to Mike Murphy.

Coming in could do 100%.

Coke in the 80s – 100%.

Charlie: Business school you learn diversification. That is bassackwards. Find a nondiversify professional investor.

Know nothings invented diversify. If you use only 20%, you miss the opportunity, instead of loading up.

Boys Town – Get toxic ads off TV. Berkshire – bad advertising – violence. Don't get it – ads are not violent.

Warren: GEICO advertising is our biggest advertiser.

Marrying well – that can be a big part of it.

Question: Should I have separate stocks in different accounts?

Warren: Add all together – not one stock in each one.

We don't do much marriage counseling.

Turn over to marriage expert.

Charlie: Ha! Ha!

Question: Will oil run out in this century? How will it play out?

Warren: Oil will not run out; it will level out, then decline slightly.

Decline curve.

86 million barrels-per-day produced.

Economy adjust – tertiary recovery in future.

Political considerations.

Can't wean world off oil.

Charlie: 200 years of industrial growth. All run out? Then use the sun.

Government policy – bad.

Warren: 25 years from now - up or down?

Charlie: Down.

Three different policy decisions for us.

Warren: Super rich pay more – middle class less.

Question: What about a food shortage?

Charlie: **Turning corn into fuel is dumb; monstrously dumb.**

Warren scoffs at the way both Clinton and Obama ask for excess profits tax on Exxon, but not on farmers getting rich off the boom in commodity prices.

Question: If at age 30, you had $1 million in bank and other job to pay bills, what would you do?

Warren: Low Cost Index Fund.

Not use a professional investor.

Croupier profits.

Pretending to be professional investors.

Do not judge by brokers here.

Kids want to keep up with the Joneses – **tell them to be frugal.**

Debt – work ethic.

Warren: Tell them to keep up with the Buffetts.

Live within your income.

Me and Charlie don't spend 105% of our income.

Be a good example - parents to children.

Question: Do Investment Bank heads know the whole business?

Warren: Some.

Gen Re has 23,000 derivative contracts – I would have had full time on it – slim or none - chance it would happen – I want none.

I am the risk officer at Berkshire.

Fannie Mae and Freddie Mac – 245-man firms – others watching them *somehow* missed their bad accounting?

Charlie: Crazy – can't allow to fail – greed and overconfidence – **it is demented to allow derivative trading**.

Warren: We want DNA against risk at the top.

Charlie: **A risk manager is just a guy who makes you feel good, while you do dumb things.**

Warren was offered Bear Stearns, but passed on it.

Warren: Good until reached for assets.

Accounting profession utterly failed us.

Solomon was trading with Mark Rich--who left the country – they were told to stop, but they did not want to.

Bear Sterns – $14.5 trillion in derivative contracts.

If bankrupt – assess them in 4-5 hours.

Two other investment banks would have gone down; nobody has to lend you money.

Every morning you wonder if people think well enough of you to lend you money.

Petro China read annual report? 2002 – no opinions – not hard to understand crude oil operation – I came to the conclusion that it was worth $100 billion – it was selling for $35 billion.

Why talk to management? They will say the company is good.

Don't overanalyze.

Buy it.

If you see a 300-pound man, you don't know his weight. You just know he is fat! (Big laugh from shareholder audience.)

They (investments) should hit you in the eye.

We have lower due-diligence costs than most companies – less problems.

We think like engineers – we want a margin of safety.

If you think Auditors know more, let them run the business.

If you use conventional due-diligence, it is a waste of time – you miss deals.

Mars wanted to deal with Berkshire.

Just say yes.

$6.5 billion available.

Our word is good even if Ben Bernanke runs off to South America with Paris Hilton.

Question: Do you have a personal relationship with Jesus?

Warren: I am agnostic. I don't know.

Question: Would a hedge fund buy Berkshire?

Warren: My stock will sell over a 12 Year period after I die; no guarantee against 600 billion dollar take over, but slim chance.

Lawyer - Make estate last a long time no problem – like telling teenage son to have a normal sex life – no problem.

Charlie: What Warren wants said at his funeral – "That is the oldest looking corpse I ever saw."

Warren: Wrigley – good return on investment.

Coke – 1.5 billion eight-ounce servings per day – a brand gets implanted in people's minds – very difficult to get out.

Branson tried Virgin Cola – failed.

We feel good about branded products.

Look at price, management, etc.

Criteria for select investment – individual - looked for good record - human qualities – ability and integrity.

We are adverse to risk.

We are not using models.

Look at new financial products.

Charlie: We are risk adverse; look for good credit.

Chief Risk Manager – computations – clobber up your own head with them.

Not dependent on others.

No leverage.

Many in this room have their entire net worth in Berkshire.

Warren: Risk management is not farmed out.

Universe of companies in head.

Can I figure it out?

Go – No go.

Not rude.

Forget it.

Said often think long time - still don't know.

Don't start to know about some business and some bonds – I know in five minutes – if I don't, I won't in five months.

We waste a lot of time on things we want to waste it on.

Question: Will Coke withdraw from Olympics?

Warren: No—it is a mistake to try to grade countries.

Charlie: Warren understates my position. **Don't pick the worst thing about a person and obsess about it.**

Question: What do you think about the coal industry short

term?

Warren: World will use more coal long-term.

We will find an alternative, but we will not find it fast.

Mid-American has put in a lot of windmills in the last five years.

China – many new coal plants.

U.S. - Not in a position to preach on it.

Charlie: People ask which will be used up first---coal or oil – I say coal. Most people don't think the way I do.

Warren: Charlie does not find comfort in numbers.

Small banks not all the same.

We owned a bank in Rockford, Illinois.

Culture of management.

We own some Wells Fargo, U.S. Bank, M&T in Buffalo.

Not all banks are immune to stupidity.

Charlie: Some small banks have been pounded down because of big banks – that is a territory that has some promise.

Warren: That is a wildly bullish statement for Charlie.

Question: What about nuclear proliferation?

Warren: The genie is out of the bottle – choke point – raw

materials and delivery system – crazy man – reduce access to materials – 6.5 billion people – a psychotic.

Progression of weapons - stone, bow and arrow, rifle, canon.

In 1945, Einstein said it changed everything except how men think – some are nuts.

We were lucky in the Cuban missile crisis.

There could be death on a scale no one has contemplated.

Most important investment is in yourself.

Most people's potential exceeds the realization.

Work on your mind.

We did not work on the body much around here.

Good habits; and Charlie – books.

Question: Buy Chicago Cubs – good investment?

Warren: Has been good – cable helped – expanded the stadium.

Psychic income to some.

Get known savings rate.

Value of country has gone up.

If you own Berkshire stock, you are automatically saving.

We (the U.S.) import $700 billion more than we export.

The average American standard-of-living will improve.

$47,000 GDP per capita – Why go to Germany?

We want more owners of old businesses to think of Berkshire when they want to monetize their company.

Charlie: Germans are very inventive.

Warren: Our problem is with mortgage financing more than the real estate bubble.

No magic – stupid things – different in future, but will happen – greed – leverage –believe in the tooth fairy – financial statements – fair value.

Read the U.S. Constitution – property rights.

Question: What do you think about Transit?

Warren: **American public does not like mass transit.**

It is unlikely there will be more people on trains and busses in the future.

Don't want to bet on change.

Charlie: You are more optimistic than me.

Climate crisis – burn up hydrocarbons – different reason than Al Gore.

Warren: Credit default swap market – $60 trillion insurance against company going bankrupt.

We have insurance – some tranches of them.

Corporate default rate will rise.

Feds stepped in at Bear Sterns and kept it from going bad.

Most volatile of instruments in the last 12 months.

Question: Problem of overnight disruption in the system?

Charlie: Could have a mess. Enormous bets that something will fail.

Question: Why no dividends?

Warren: Do you believe you can create more than $1 of value for every $1 retained?

If the time comes, and it will some day, then we will pay it out in dividends.

Charlie: Saint Augustine, "God give me chastity, but not yet."

California power coal plants near Grand Canyon.

Question: Will you buy businesses in India or China?

Warren: Odds are against it – we will buy small ones with subsidiaries.

Question: What are two or three influences on you?

Warren: Father, who you marry, Ben Graham, David Dodd.

Most important job as a parent is teacher to your children.

Teach by what you do, not what you say.

Charlie: For me I learn from reading – talker is bad.

Warren: Book recommendation: *The Intelligent Investor.*

Question: Executive compensation too high? What can I do?

Warren: Institutional owners can withhold votes and issue statement to press.

Ben Graham said investors are a bunch of sheep.

England has a lot of class warfare – 90% tax rate ruined the country; politics of envy is very bad.

Question: Drug company-pipeline?

Warren: Don't know.

Question: Group bought at a reasonable price?

Warren: Reasonable multiple – China – invested in Petro China.

Valued at $35 - $40 billion to $100 billion. It went to $275 or $300 billion. Not undervalued; after we sold, it went up.

China economy coming up – political system did not let it go up – now it is.

Question: Copy qualities?

Warren: Don Keogh, Tom Murphy.

Charlie: Confucius – emphasis on reverence for elderly males.

Question: What is the future hope for Berkshire?

Warren: Hope is for decent performance for Berkshire and to keep the culture.

It is the best home for a big family-owned business.

You can sell to Berkshire and keep the business like it is.

Charlie: Berkshire exemplar.

Warren: Oldest living managers.

Chapter 9

The following is a summary of the bold items throughout the various chapters.

Absolute move-up is based on earnings and interest rates.

We try not to do anything difficult.

Time is the enemy of a poor business; it is the friend of a good business.

We buy stock; we don't want to sell.

Our insurance business is the most important. I said many years ago that it would be.

"I AM PROUD TO SAY WE HAVE <u>NO</u> MISSION STATEMENT!"

The secret to life is weak competition.

Think about things that are important and knowable.

Price, action, and volatility have nothing to do with what we do.

We step over 1-foot bars; we do not try to jump over 8-foot bars.

How it is taught in business school is incoherent – it is a stupid question - we are drowning in cash.

We never had many stock recommendations from analysts; we don't want them.

We look for the fat pitch.

You will do well if you buy at a good price and the business does well.

They (Tech) are 8-foot bars. I can't clear it. Better to swing at easy pitches.

Question: Small cap vs large cap? We don't look at that, or sectors, or stuff that gets merchandised.

Talent is a scarce commodity. When you find it – good.

Best business - cash comes in, you don't have to spend cash to expand.

Question: What is the criteria used to select a stock or business? Understand the product.

Earning power good and getting better.

Good people.

Good price.

Simple, but not easy.

Know what you don't know.

If the market goes down, we like it. We can buy more!

We (Charlie and I) are wired to be good at capital allocation.

We don't pay any attention to Beta. The focus is 10 years from now.

Question: What is the difference between good business and bad business? A good business keeps throwing up easy decisions. In a bad business—they are all tough decisions.

The trick is to get more in quality than you pay in price.

A lot of people will say they are from Nebraska for status reasons.

We don't look at the market. We look at individual businesses.

We only buy value.

Money piles up; then we pile in.

You only have to get rich once. Don't risk losing it.

Success in investing – retained earnings and float determine success.

It is not a problem to have a pile of money.

We have no PR department.

Look at your area of expertise. We don't like to nibble. We want to take big gulps.

Money makes little difference after a certain amount.

My life is similar to a college student (except travel).

Share of market –Share of mind. Good feeling about product.

PE ratio now is unimportant if looking at 10 to 15 years out.

Question: Analyst coverage? Don't care.

keep investing on a regular basis.

Would bet on Gates.

Willing to trade *big* payoff for *certain* payoff.

Investment is about valuing a business.

Goal is to grow float fast with low cost.

Growth in intrinsic value of Berkshire will be affected by growth of float.

Question: How can I make $30 billion? Start young--or live to be old. Start with the A's in Moody's. Do your own research. Look for undervalued stocks. Learn what you know and what you don't know. Don't look for consensus. The first look is the hardest. Be rational. Under spend your income.

A dumb mistake refreshes your attention.

Question: Is management bright or stupid? Big moat – need less management. Have to understand business.

You are not sufficiently critical of academics doing standard deviation.

We have done fewer dumb things.

Liberal arts teaches one to feel like a victim.

Winners – Good franchise, management, distribution system, float.

Coke – huge potential in China.

Emerging market funds equals nonsense.

Sectors - same – nonsense.

Early investment and promotion we understand. Internet VC funding – we have no interest. We will not turn your money over to someone else to manage.

Question: Invest in high tech VC? Call Bill Gates.

Go away for 10 years - put your money in one company - which one? Bill Gates said Coke.

In many companies, there is a large group of people whose importance is measured by meddling in the affairs of the people doing the work.

There is no distinction between growth and value in our minds.

Buy value - expect growth - very simple!

All intelligent investing is value investing.

The amount of cash a stock can disgorge = price or worth.

Newspapers are threatened by the Internet.

We don't have a set PE ratio for buy - no buy.

We want a great stream of cash estimate over 10 or 20 years.

Question: Are you going to buy Tech? We will not buy anything we don't understand.

We do not look at the stock price and feel poor or rich. We look at the business and feel richer or poorer.

The stock price will eventually follow the value of the company.

Focus on what is knowable and important.

We would do a large dividend.

We would love to find a business to buy that is selling for ½ what it is worth.

We love our jobs!

Do they the maneger love the business or love the money?

To hire an investment banker to evaluate businesses to buy is idiocy. If we cannot evaluate it, we are in trouble.

Compared to an e-retailer, Insurance is far superior.

Question: What about Freddie Mac? Too much political undertones.

If organization lies at the top, employees adopt that as their policy, too.

Don't talk to analysts.

It is a waste of our managers' time to talk to analysts.

We have no Compensation Consultant.

We have no HR Department.

We have no Investors' Relations Committee.

Bill Gates is the smartest person. He can do your job – not you his.

Did Bill put you up to this?

Temperament is all important.

It does not require extended intellect, but extended discipline.

If you find one, go big. To diversify is wrong.

Asset Allocation is merchandising. You don't need them.

You don't have to do hard stuff in investing.

We don't do a lot of leverage. It is the one thing that can

keep you from playing out your hand.

We bought it because it was very very, cheap.

The low cost producer is a good bet.

Average person who buys an IPO gets creamed.

No credit card debt.

Leverage is bad.

Berkshire is in a strong position with cash.

We have $44 billion in cash.

Intelligence, energy, integrity – if they have no integrity, we want dumb and lazy – do they love the money or love the business?

Need unpleasantness to buy in a large company.

Got interested at age 7 – wasted my time before that.

I read a lot – every book in the Omaha Public Library on the stock market.

I read the Graham book while at the University of Nebraska at age 19.

It is a huge advantage to start young in any field.

It requires temperament, not I.Q.

Develop a framework.

Look for opportunities that fit within it.

Don't act every day.

If you enjoy it, you will do well.

Petro China - Paid $400 million; now it is worth $1.2 billion.

We like to buy businesses with untapped pricing power – like See's Candy.

We have the best group of shareholders.

Buy a good business – selling at a cheap price.

At $27 million, (a beach front house) I'd rather stare at my bathtub.

We Don't own Freddie or Fannie now.

Merger of Berkshire Hathaway and Microsoft? I keep hinting, but it does not work.

Don't do asset allocation.

If a thing is not worth doing at all, it is not worth doing well.

See--he is Ben Franklin!

We have no group Vice Presidents, Headquarters Directives, HR Department, PR Department, or Law Department in Omaha.

There is a bubble in real estate now.

REITS – overpriced now.

Buy a company so good an idiot could run it, because some day one will!

Amount of credit being used is way too heavy.

We have the best Board in the country.

We will stay within our circle of competence.

It was like putting $100 million in a bushel basket and setting it on fire (bad deal).

Throw it into the "too hard" pile and move on.

Charlie: Stupid and dishonorable accountants let genie out of the bottle.

Know what you don't know.

Know your circle of competence.

We know the edge of our circle of competence.

Petro China – $400 million in - now worth $2 billion.

Bad lending – Dumb lending - plus terrible accounting.

We have $37 billion in cash.

We want $10 billion as a rule.

Warren: In aggregate, investment professional does not add value; however $140 billion is spent on it every year.

Well, I (Warren) made a couple billion dollars with it. If it's not a big thing to him (Charlie), he can give his share to me! (Big laugh from the audience.)

Investment is not tough – you need the courage of your convictions.

You only need one good idea.

I look for something very mispriced that I understand.

Ben Graham said, "You are neither right nor wrong because somebody agrees or disagrees with you."

Knowable and important – market is there to serve you – not instruct you.

You can't miss.

Look at earnings.

With many complex tasks - do the easy ones first – no brainers.

Day trading is gambling.

Gambling is a tax on ignorance.

State lottery – government preys on the weakness of its citizenry.

Great businesses don't need a large margin of safety.

A fat business you know (a good business).

Buy a good business at a reasonable price.

Look for low distribution cost.

Low frictional cost.

Intrinsic value is based on the future cash of the business discounted, back to the present.

Aesop – 600 BC – A bird in the hand is worth two in the bush.

Fundamentals of investing.

Know when know.

Know when don't.

Most ideas go in the too-hard pile.

We can recognize one foot bars.

We can step over one foot bars.

Get a program.

Don't do anything where you can lose a lot.

A good business will carry a bad manager.

A good manager can't fix a bad business.

It is stupid   Why would you put your food in your car to run it?

I tried 20 different businesses by the time I (Warren) got out of high school.

Business success vs different variables – best correlation with the age you start your first business – the younger the better.

Under- spend your income, and then invest the difference.

If it has a big labor cost and can be built overseas, we don't want it.

Turning corn into fuel is dumb; monstrously dumb.

Tell them to be frugal.

Live within your income.

I (Warren) am the risk officer at Berkshire.

It is demented to allow derivative trading.

A Risk Manager is just a guy who makes you feel good, while you do dumb things.

If you see a 300 pound man, you don't know his weight. You just know he is fat! (Big laugh from shareholder audience.)

They (investments) should hit you in the eye.

We think like engineers – we want a margin of safety.

Don't pick the worst thing about a person and obsess about it.

Some small banks have been pounded down because of big banks – that is a territory that has some promise. That is a wildly bullish statement for Charlie.

If you own Berkshire stock, you are automatically saving.

No magic – stupid things – different in future, but will happen – greed – leverage –believe in the tooth fairy.

American public does not like mass transit.

It is unlikely there will be more people on trains and buses in the future.

1998: Bill and Warren at Dairy Queen in Omaha

1998: Warren and Cheryl at Dairy Queen in Omaha

2000: Cheryl and Warren at Borsheims in Omaha

2000: Bill and Warren at Borsheims in Omaha

2005: Berkshire hat at 2005 Convention

2007: Bill with cutouts of Warren and Charlie in Exhibit Hall

2007: Cheryl with cutouts of Warren and Charlie in Exhibit Hall

2007: Cheryl and Longhorn Steer at Justin Boots Exhibit

2007: Bill and Longhorn Steer at Justin Boots Exhibit

2007: Bill and Cheryl in front of Johns Manville racing car

2007: Bill with Marla Gottschalk, CEO of Pampered Chef

2007: Berkshire hat at 2007 Convention